MW01181198

Pepperdine University
Malibu, California

Written by Steve Pinkerton

Edited by Adam Burns, Kimberly Moore, and Jon Skindzier

Layout by Meghan Dowdell

Additional contributions by Omid Gohari,
Christina Koshzow, Chris Mason, Joey Rahimi,
and Luke Skurman

ISBN # 1-4274-0110-1
ISSN # 1551-0595
© Copyright 2006 College Prowler
All Rights Reserved
Printed in the U.S.A.
www.collegeprowler.com

Last updated 5/16/06

Special Thanks To: Babs Carryer, Andy Hannah, LaunchCyte, Tim O'Brien, Bob Sehlinger, Thomas Emerson, Andrew Skurman, Barbara Skurman, Bert Mann, Dave Lehman, Daniel Fayock, Chris Babyak, The Donald H. Jones Center for Entrepreneurship, Terry Slease, Jerry McGinnis, Bill Ecenberger, Idie McGinty, Kyle Russell, Jacque Zaremba, Larry Winderbaum, Roland Allen, Jon Reider, Team Evankovich, Lauren Varacalli, Abu Noaman, Jason Putorti, Mark Exler, Daniel Steinmeyer, Jared Cohon, Gabriela Oates, David Koegler, and Glen Meakem.

Bounce-Back Team: Alejandro Ramirez, Elizabeth Reinking, and Taneekia Collymore.

College Prowler®
5001 Baum Blvd.
Suite 750
Pittsburgh, PA 15213

Phone: 1-800-290-2682
Fax: 1-800-772-4972
E-Mail: info@collegeprowler.com
Web Site: www.collegeprowler.com

Welcome to College Prowler®

During the writing of College Prowler's guidebooks, we felt it was critical that our content was unbiased and unaffiliated with any college or university. We think it's important that our readers get honest information and a realistic impression of the student opinions on any campus—that's why if any aspect of a particular school is terrible, we (unlike a campus brochure) intend to publish it. While we do keep an eye out for the occasional extremist—the cheerleader or the cynic—we take pride in letting the students tell it like it is. We strive to create a book that's as representative as possible of each particular campus. Our books cover both the good and the bad, and whether the survey responses point to recurring trends or a variation in opinion, these sentiments are directly and proportionally expressed through our guides.

College Prowler guidebooks are in the hands of students throughout the entire process of their creation. Because you can't make student-written guides without the students, we have students at each campus who help write, randomly survey their peers, edit, layout, and perform accuracy checks on every book that we publish. From the very beginning, student writers gather the most up-to-date stats, facts, and inside information on their colleges. They fill each section with student quotes and summarize the findings in editorial reviews. In addition, each school receives a collection of letter grades (A through F) that reflect student opinion and help to represent contentment, prominence, or satisfaction for each of our 20 specific categories. Just as in grade school, the higher the mark the more content, more prominent, or more satisfied the students are with the particular category.

Once a book is written, additional students serve as editors and check for accuracy even more extensively. Our bounce-back team—a group of randomly selected students who have no involvement with the project—are asked to read over the material in order to help ensure that the book accurately expresses every aspect of the university and its students. This same process is applied to the 200-plus schools College Prowler currently covers. Each book is the result of endless student contributions, hundreds of pages of research and writing, and countless hours of hard work. All of this has led to the creation of a student information network that stretches across the nation to every school that we cover. It's no easy accomplishment, but it's the reason that our guides are such a great resource.

When reading our books and looking at our grades, keep in mind that every college is different and that the students who make up each school are not uniform—as a result, it is important to assess schools on a case-by-case basis. Because it's impossible to summarize an entire school with a single number or description, each book provides a dialogue, not a decision, that's made up of 20 different topics and hundreds of student quotes. In the end, we hope that this guide will serve as a valuable tool in your college selection process. Enjoy!

OMID GOHARI ◯ CHRISTINA KOSHZOW ◯ CHRIS MASON ◯ JOEY RAHIMI ◯ LUKE SKURMAN ◯
The College Prowler Team

PEPPERDINE UNIVERSITY
Table of Contents

Introduction from the Author

I first encountered Pepperdine University at one of those cheesy college fairs that high school juniors all attend to get an excused absence for the day. As a group of us wandered toward an alluring blue and orange booth, a classmate of mine explained rather dubiously that the school it was promoting was in Southern California somewhere, and that it was full of hot Catholic girls or Mormons or something. He was sketchy on the fine points. I flipped through the dazzling Pepperdine brochure for a moment, replaced it on the pile, and briefly entertained the notion of frolicking with beautiful, spiritual women in the renowned Southern California sun, the cool waves lapping teasingly at our sandy feet. Something snapped me out of this reverie, though, and I proceeded to forget all about Pepperdine—until a fateful July night that following summer. As I earnestly mulled over my college options by watching *Saturday Night Live* reruns, a sketch came on concerning a young UCLA grad (Jimmy Fallon) at a job interview. His potential employer, played by host Steve Buscemi, seemed impressed at first; his smile soon faded, however, as he scanned the applicant's resume. "What's this?" he demanded. "Yucka? Uckla?" When the young man clarified where he had recently graduated, a confused Buscemi responded, "Why didn't you go to Pepperdine? I've heard of Pepperdine."

Like Buscemi's character, a lot of people have heard of Pepperdine—its basketball team, its idyllic setting, or its well-heeled and attractive student body—but still a general fogginess pervades the public's understanding. It is its own little universe, a sheltered community far removed from the stereotypical atmosphere one expects of that place commonly known as "college." And while Pepperdine keeps the outside world from intruding on its students' collective consciousness, it also remains largely obscure in the public mind (note how often the word "bubble" finds its way into student quotes). "Isn't that a Catholic school?" someone will ask. Or: "Pepperdine, eh? Talk about a party school!" Or: "Isn't that one of them private country clubs?" The stereotypes are endless. Of course, there are many valid ways of looking at Pepperdine. Most conspicuous are the appealing aesthetics of surf, palm trees, and bikinis. Then there are the small class sizes, good teachers, and great international programs that comprise the core of Pepperdine's esteemed academics. Finally, there is the Christian affiliation that delights many among the student body, even as it annoys others. I certainly could have used more clarification on all of these things four years ago when, armed with the impressions I had gleaned from a daydream at a college fair, an obscure comedy sketch on TV, and the oblivious insights of friends and acquaintances, I made the rash but momentous decision to apply to Pepperdine University. I got accepted and went on to have an immensely satisfying college experience, but it would have been nice at the outset to know a bit more about my school. The contrasting and objective student perspectives this guidebook presents on all aspects of life at Pepperdine should allow you to see the school in a more three-dimensional and accurate way, and thus allow you to decide whether the real Pepperdine—not just the one in the brochures—is really a good fit for you.

Steve Pinkerton, Author
Pepperdine University

By the Numbers

General Information:

Pepperdine University
24255 Pacific Coast Highway
Malibu, CA 90263

Control:
Private

Academic Calendar:
Semester

Religious Affiliation:
Church of Christ

Founded:
1937 by George Pepperdine

Web Site:
www.pepperdine.edu

Main Phone:
(310) 506-4000

Admissions Phone:
(310) 506-4392

Student Body

**Full-Time
Undergraduates:**
2,651

**Part-Time
Undergraduates:**
550

**Total Male
Undergraduates:**
1,387

**Total Female
Undergraduates:**
1,814

Admissions

Overall Acceptance Rate:
27%

Total Applicants:
6,447

Total Acceptances:
1,555

Freshman Enrollment:
653

Yield (% of admitted students who actually enroll):
42%

Early Decision Available?
No

Early Action Available?
No

Regular Decision Deadline:
January 15

Regular Decision Notification:
April 1

Must-Reply-By Date:
May 1

Applicants Placed on Waiting List:
331

Applicants Accepted from Waiting List:
147

Students Enrolled from Waiting List:
65

Transfer Applications Received:
482

Transfer Applications Accepted:
86

Transfer Students Enrolled:
114

Transfer Application Acceptance Rate:
23.7%

Common Application Accepted?
Yes

Supplemental Forms?
Yes

Admissions E-Mail:
admission-seaver@pepperdine.edu

Admissions Web Site:
www.seaver.pepperdine.edu/admission

SAT I or ACT Required?
Either

SAT I Range (25th–75th Percentile):
1110–1310

SAT I Verbal Range (25th–75th Percentile):
550–650

**SAT I Math Range
(25th–75th Percentile):**
560–660

**Top 10% of
High School Class:**
42%

Retention Rate:
88%

Application Fee:
$55

Financial Information

Tuition:
$30,860

Students Who Received Aid:
57%

Room and Board:
$9,100

Financial Aid Forms Deadline:
February 15

Books and Supplies:
$800

Financial Aid Phone:
(310) 506-4301

**Average Need-Based
Financial Aid Package:**
$26,482

Financial Aid E-Mail:
admission-seaver@
pepperdine.edu

**Students Who Applied
for Financial Aid:**
66%

Financial Aid Web Site:
*www.pepperdine.edu/
admission/financialaid*

Academics

The Lowdown On...
Academics

Degrees Awarded:

Bachelor

Master

Post-Master Certificate

First Professional

Doctorate

Most Popular Majors:

36% Business, Management, and Marketing

16% Communication and Journalism

10% Psychology

8% Social Sciences

5% Liberal Arts and Humanities

Undergraduate Schools:

The George L. Graziadio School of Business and Management (upper-division)

Seaver College

Full-Time Faculty:

390 (52%)

Faculty with Terminal Degree:

96%

Student-to-Faculty Ratio:

12:1

Average Course Load:

4 courses

Graduation Rates:

Four-Year: 68%

Five-Year: 76%

Six-Year: 77%

Special Degree Options

Pepperdine students can create their own custom "contract majors" by completing unique curricula according to the guidelines of their specific divisions.

AP Test Score Requirements

Possible credit for scores of 3 or better in most subjects (score of 4 required in German, French, and physics).

IB Test Score Requirements

Possible credit for scores of 5 or better in higher level courses.

Sample Academic Clubs

Accounting Society, Alpha Delta Sigma (advertising), Golden Key, Eta Psi, Pi Delta Phi (French), Phi Alpha Delta (pre-law), Phi Delta Epsilon (pre-med), PRSSA (public relations), Psi Chi (psychology), SHRM (human resources and management), Sigma Delta Pi (Spanish), Sigma Tau Delta (English), Sports Medicine Club, Students in Free Enterprise

Best Places to Study

Howard A. White Center, Payson Library, and Waves Café

Did You Know?

Pepperdine is particularly proud of its great international programs; **over half of all Pepperdine students travel abroad** in at least one of these programs during the course of their college study.

Students Speak Out On...
Academics

"Most professors are pretty cool. They're demanding. If you're looking for a cakewalk, you're going to the wrong school. It's the luck of the draw whether you get the good ones or the bad ones."

Q "The teachers at Pepperdine are, as a rule, people who actually want to be teaching. Because it's a small university, **teachers aren't really there just so they can do their self-fulfilling research**. The majority of my teachers have been helpful and enthusiastic about their field. I always feel totally comfortable going to talk to professors about getting extra help or having questions answered. A lot of professors will have their classes to dinner, which is at first a little awkward, but it ends up being a fun college experience that people at large schools don't get to have."

Q "**I found most teachers to be easily accessible** and more than willing to help you with the class and its related material—except for the general education classes with hundreds of people in them. Teachers in these classes seemed annoyed with student questions, and they'd shun their TAs."

Q "Ironically, my most straightforward and non-religious class was religion. **Expect lots of ex-pastors for professors**."

Q "**Some of the English teachers are wackos** (which goes along with the major), but most of them really want you to succeed and do well, and with the small class sizes, they have the ability to give one-on-one help. I even had a professor who would cry while reading Shakespeare. Religion classes were not interesting—ever. They are, however, required."

Q "As I'm sure is true of most schools, **the classes and the teachers can be hit-or-miss**. For the most part, I have had kind and intelligent teachers leading worthwhile to excellent classes—but I have also had a handful of teachers who are very poor, grouchy, or extremely arrogant."

Q "Most of the teachers have their quirks, and **some are downright quirky**. All take a sincere interest in their students' learning."

Q "**The teachers are excellent**. The key is having regular meetings with the teachers outside of class."

Q "The teachers are friendly and are always willing to help. They will **invite you over to their houses for dinner**, and they'll give you their home numbers if you ever have any questions at all. They can do this because of the small class sizes. Also, they all live on or close to campus."

Q "**The teachers at Pepperdine are okay**. I have taken classes at a community college during the summer, and the teachers there were a lot better, as far as being open-minded and sensitive to the needs of their students. But then again, I haven't had every teacher on campus, so this cannot be entirely accurate."

Q "All of my teachers have been great. They all know what they're talking about, and they have a lot of enthusiasm for what they are teaching. They really want to see you succeed. **My largest class this whole year was 30 students, and most of my classes had about 20 people** in them. It was awesome. There are only a few lecture-style classes taught; everything else is very personal."

Q "All the teachers I had, with the exception of one, were great. They are always willing to help you and are understanding in every way possible. It is a tough school, and classes are challenging, but **the academic experience is certainly rewarding**."

Q "The teachers I had at Pepperdine were all very different from each other. Some were conservative religious professors who were very academic in the way they structured their courses, while others were more liberal professors who tried to stimulate their students in interesting, innovative ways. For example, I wrote a full screenplay during my junior year. Across the board, **I received a well-rounded perspective of the discipline I was studying**."

Q "Several of my professors have **remained close friends** of mine since I graduated, and one is even a peer now."

Q "I found most of my classes interesting and challenging. Of course, how challenged you are depends on how challenged you want to be. Just skimming by and doing almost nothing is an option, but it doesn't lead to a very interesting experience. The general education classes got a bit tedious by the end there, but **every class had some element of intrigue**."

The College Prowler Take On...
Academics

Pepperdine people seem genuinely satisfied with their instructors and their courses. Class sizes matter more than an incoming student might expect, and Pepperdine offers some of the smallest, most intimate classes in California. Students unanimously praise the one-on-one interaction that Pepperdine teachers tend to promote, just as they lament the two or three lecture-oriented general education courses they may have endured over their four years in Malibu. Whether one appreciates the religious tilt of many Pepperdine courses will most likely depend on one's own beliefs. However, most consider the Christian emphasis to be, at its worst, only mildly tedious or distracting.

Pepperdine emphasizes the importance of teaching over research, so professors are invariably available, approachable, smart, and happy to help their students with just about anything. A result of this warm and fuzzy student-professor relationship is that a lot of classes seem, well, not particularly demanding; one wonders whether more expectations and harder assignments might provoke, in turn, more learning. Most students don't complain too much about all of that, though. Also, the administration aims its funding predominantly toward its business and natural science programs, at times leaving its other departments out in the cold—despite Pepperdine's self-description as a liberal arts school. Incoming students should definitely consider the four-semester Great Books program, which not only introduces students to the history of Western thought, it also satisfies a lot of GE requirements (even math!). Also, the excellent international programs are an opportunity not to be missed. Those who can manage the expense of spending a semester, or a year, in Florence or Buenos Aires or any of the other popular Pepperdine destinations, should do just that.

B

The College Prowler® Grade on
Academics: B

A high Academics grade generally indicates that professors are knowledgeable, accessible, and genuinely interested in their students' welfare. Other determining factors include class size, how well professors communicate, and whether or not classes are engaging.

Local Atmosphere

The Lowdown On...
Local Atmosphere

Region:
Pacific Coast

City, State:
Malibu, California

Setting:
Suburban

**Distance from
Los Angeles:**
20 minutes

**Distance from
San Francisco:**
Six hours

Points of Interest:
Disneyland
Hollywood
Magic Mountain
Universal Studios

➡

Closest Shopping Malls:

Malibu shops

Promenade

Santa Monica, on 3rd Street

Closest Movie Theater:

Malibu Theater

Malibu Shopping Ctr., Malibu

(310) 456-6990

Major Sports Teams:

Angels (baseball)

Kings (hockey)

Dodgers (baseball)

Lakers (basketball)

Mighty Ducks (hockey)

City Web Sites

www.ci.malibu.ca.us

www.malibu.org

Did You Know?

5 Fun Facts about Malibu:

- **The Chumash Indian word malibu means "noisy waters"** (better than that other sleepy California town, Lompoc, whose name means "stagnant waters").

- It hosts the annual **Malibu International Film Festival**, as well as the annual Malibu Chili Cook-Off. Pepperdine's frats and sororities often join in the latter competition.

- **A mysterious surfer organization** known as "Malibu Locals Only," or MLO, protects its home turf by picking fights with non-Malibu surfing citizens and by spray-painting its three ominous initials onto cement surfaces.

- *Baywatch* was filmed on Malibu's voluptuous golden beaches.

- On several nights between March and August, at high tide, the Southern California coastline becomes besieged by "grunion runs," the **bizarre spawning ritual of thousands of little translucent fishes called grunion**. These grunion runs—the timing of which is based on the moon cycle and can be predicted long in advance—make for very interesting marine biology field trips.

Famous Malibu Residents:

You name it! Everyone who is anyone in the entertainment industry has at least one home in Malibu. Don't be surprised if you find yourself driving alongside Pierce Brosnan's Aston Martin, or if you run into that guy who played TV's MacGyver in the cereal aisle at a Ralphs grocery store.

Local Slang:

The 'Bu – Abbreviated form of Malibu.

Chill – Used as an adjective or a verb, as in "I was chillin' with this really chill girl."

Plus the hippest and latest surfer culture expressions—nothing you haven't heard on MTV.

Students Speak Out On...
Local Atmosphere

"Malibu is a very nice, sophisticated town. It's right next to the beach, which is really cool. The campus is almost like a resort. You don't really think of it as a school when you first get there."

Q "The sun is usually shining, the kids are usually smiling, and **the surf is usually doing something worthwhile**."

Q "**I found Malibu nightlife to be excruciatingly boring**. It includes two bars in town and house parties. There are no cool frat parties due to the lack of frat houses. The one thing Malibu does not lack is beaches; there are many beautiful ones that I would highly recommend."

Q "Malibu has a feel that I don't think can be matched by any other city in the nation. Mostly, the word you're searching for to describe the atmosphere is 'rich.' **An absolute breeding ground for celebrities**, it's common to see people like Mel Gibson, Pamela Anderson, or Justin Timberlake at the grocery store on weekends— something you don't get at many other universities."

Q "Pepperdine is a pretty isolated place, tucked back next to the coast. If you want to have contact with other universities, your only real bet is to go to the sporting events, or meet through Greek organizations. **No one would ever call Malibu a happening place**, because other than going to the beach, there is nothing to do."

Q "The only place open past 10 p.m. is the grocery store. That being said, **the bright lights of LA are within a 30-minute drive**, and if you don't mind the distance, there's no end to the activities available."

Q "Take away the Pepperdine campus, and **you've got yourself a dead town**. Don't even think about not having a car; you'll thank me when you don't have to cross two major highways to get to the supermarket."

Q "**The beach gets way too cold, so don't envision yourself studying by the waves into November**. Think summer school. That's the only way to study and catch some rays. Malibu Yo' (the local yogurt shop) is a must, but remember that frozen yogurt is not a major food group."

Q "In terms of things not to miss, Third Street Promenade in Santa Monica is likely where you'll spend a great deal of time your freshman year. It's a street set aside for pedestrians, lined with good restaurants and better shopping, and **within walking distance of the beach** and the Santa Monica Pier. By junior year, you'll be over it—but the first few times you go, it's just fantastic."

Q "The locals can often exude their distaste for college students ruining their little neighborhood, but besides that, Malibu is small and quaint. Annoyingly, though, **it's a minimum 20-minute drive from anywhere**. Other universities are not really present (read: isolated). Personally, I say stay away from the Malibu Inn, and don't fall into visiting the same places over and over."

Q "Malibu itself is gorgeous, but the people are extremely standoffish. **I had a very hard time interacting with older Malibu residents** who seem to have preconceived notions regarding Pepperdine students. I think the "college" scene has a bad reputation among the quiet Malibu residents who want to keep to themselves, with little to no interaction with others outside of their social circles."

Q "It is a gorgeous campus; you will not find one that is any nicer than Pepperdine. **It's right on the ocean**, with most of the classrooms affording spectacular views."

Q "There are other universities nearby, but Malibu and Pepperdine tend to remain **enclosed in an unacknowledged bubble**. It's sort of inconvenient to leave the area for an extended period of time, though it's cool to join the social scene of UCLA or USC occasionally."

Q "**Stuff to visit: anywhere in Santa Monica**. The Getty is a beautiful museum with a beautiful view of LA. I very rarely explored Los Angeles, as I was a bit intimidated by the traffic flow myself, but I've heard that LA has several cool things to do."

Q "**Do not see the La Brea Tar Pits**. They are a waste of time."

Q "Malibu has some great hangout spots, but the town shuts down early. **It can be a stuck-up town**. This is LA, and everyone is into image. Everyone is either an aspiring actor or model. Everyone wants to be part of the entertainment industry. Lots of people come to Pepperdine with the preconceived notion that they're going to get 'discovered,' or something like that. It won't happen in Malibu."

Q "Malibu is small. Everything is about 45 minutes away. **In LA, you have to drive literally 45 minutes to get anywhere**, but you get used to it. Santa Monica is fun. People usually go to USC or UCLA to party, because Pepperdine is virtually dead on the weekends. The whole 'no drinking' thing plays a big part in that."

Q "There is really nothing special about Malibu, except big houses. Other than that, there is **really good shopping in Santa Monica** and through the canyon."

Q "The atmosphere is pretty nice, and it is always fun to rub shoulders with celebrities. When you go to dinner in Malibu, there's a good chance you'll see someone famous. I've seen a ton of celebs at Ralphs grocery store. However, **Malibu is not what I'd call a college town**. UCLA, USC, and Loyola are all within 30 minutes, so there's a lot of college kids pretty close. There's a ton of stuff to visit. Half of the rooms on campus have an ocean view. Mine did. LA has an endless list of things to do."

Q "The Malibu atmosphere is way chill. There's only one grocery store, so the famous people have to shop there. **You'll definitely get your fill of celebrities**. UCLA and USC are down the road. Kids party there a lot. Loyola Marymount is close, too. There's a ton of stuff to visit: Hollywood Boulevard, Sunset Boulevard, Rodeo Drive, the Malibu Chili Cook-Off, the Malibu Country Mart, Zuma Beach, Disneyland, and anything in San Diego. Hawaii is a four-hour flight, Vegas is a 45-minute flight, and ski trips are popular."

Q "Malibu is relaxing, but **you need to drive to do things**."

The College Prowler Take On...
Local Atmosphere

Differences in student opinion regarding Malibu probably tell more about the priorities and prior experiences of the opinion-holders than they do about the town itself. To some, Malibu is an irritating 20-minute drive from anything interesting to see or do; while to others, it's a mere 20-minute drive from fabulous Santa Monica or a thrilling half-hour jaunt away from LA. Some scoff at the trappings of wealth and celebrity that Malibu so quaintly celebrates, while others head down the hill to the Coffee Bean to sit and watch for movie stars. Everyone can agree, though, that Malibu is a truly unique place to go to college—surreal, really—and a genuine experience.

The 'Bu is a sleepy little enclave for the fabulously wealthy, into which Pepperdine University has rather awkwardly asserted itself. It's no place for a college student, especially one on a budget, to have a particularly wild time after dusk. On the upside, it is an undeniably beautiful environment for study, reflection, or any sport involving wetsuit-clad human beings trying to tame a vast, violent body of saltwater.

The College Prowler® Grade on

Local
Atmosphere: B

A high Local Atmosphere grade indicates that the area surrounding campus is safe and scenic. Other factors include nearby attractions, proximity to other schools, and the town's attitude toward students.

Safety & Security

The Lowdown On...
Safety & Security

Number of Pepperdine Public Safety Officers:
38

Emergency Phone:
(310) 506-4700

Safety Services:
Designated Driver Program
Emergency phones
Escort
Operation ID
Wave Watch

Health Services:
First aid, health insurance, STD testing (including free and anonymous HIV testing), prescription refills, eating disorder treatment, lab work, referrals, sports medicine, dermatology, allergy and flu shots, travel medicine, immunizations, and nutritional counseling

Health Center Office Hours:
Monday–Friday
8 a.m.–5 p.m.

Did You Know?

Between the years 2002 and 2005, students **reported 63 burglaries, three sexual assaults, and six car thefts**. Public Safety "wrote up" 259 students for drinking (nine of which were for off-campus incidents), 49 students for drug abuse, and eight students for weapons possession.

Students Speak Out On...
Safety & Security

{ **"The security is great on campus. The area surrounding the school is very nice, making you feel safe at all times."**

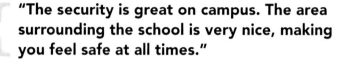

"I've always felt extremely safe at Pepperdine. It's a totally self-enclosed campus, and the only two entrances are monitored 24 hours a day by guards. Students joke that it's not hard to sneak on campus, and that's pretty much true, but I've never heard of any incidents that would make me feel uncomfortable."

"I've never had any concerns about my safety or security. **As long as you use common sense** and don't leave your laptop in the middle of campus, I don't think you have anything to worry about."

"Sure, you'll hear lots of complaints about Public Safety, but for some reason, **their presence made me feel warm and fuzzy during lonely Malibu nights**. It also felt good knowing that the entire Pepperdine universe was a gated community."

"Pepperdine is safe enough; **sometimes Public Safety can be overly cautious**."

"**Public Safety is often overbearing**, but I suppose as a result of that, I never feel endangered, really."

"We have very, very good security on campus. Campus police always patrol the roads, and two main gates close off the campus. **Any crimes on campus are people stealing stuff**, like my little barbeque grill last semester. I guess someone couldn't wait to grill a steak."

Q "Pepperdine is probably one of the safest campuses in the country. The actual 'learning areas'—the dorms and cafeteria—are up on a hill, above the beach. Because Pepperdine is so small, the only threats I can fathom you would encounter would be from actual students themselves. Yet, as an assurance, you must take into consideration that these students have decided to attend a **Christian college where Christian values are upheld**. Violence, vandalism, and other criminal activities are obviously not any of the values Pepperdine supports. At the entrance to the campus, at the base of the hill, is a security check-in booth where visitors must check in. The nearest major city is 20 minutes away, and Malibu is not known for problems with the law."

Q "The campus feels very safe. It is well lit, there are usually people out at all times of the day and night, and the campus security team is close by. My one complaint about campus security is that **they seem always to be around when they shouldn't be** and are never around when they should be. Be aware that if you need a ride from them, it will take about an hour for them to get you (even if you are only a few buildings away from them)."

Q "Totally safe. Well, I shouldn't feel so safe, since our security isn't too strict. I think they are a bit relaxed because they know it's a safe campus, too. **It's so isolated that it's safe**. However, someone once got into my suite, which was really scary. They were banging on the door for my roommate. It was that easy for them to get in."

Q "Safety is good and always improving. Public Safety is constantly running laps around dorm roads. **Plus, the firemen are drop-dead gorgeous**!"

The College Prowler Take On...
Safety & Security

Whatever concerns Pepperdine students may have about their chosen school, safety obviously is not one of them. Every so often, one will hear of a theft or two—last year a bunch of laptop computers disappeared from the communications building, for example—but hardly anyone ever expresses much anxiety over the security of their belongings. Certainly, no one seems worried about his or her own physical safety.

Malibu is not a dangerous town, so Pepperdine hardly needs to take many precautions. It takes them anyway, though. Security guards monitor the gated entrances to campus 24 hours a day, and Public Safety vehicles are everywhere, always. Sprinkled throughout campus are emergency phones marked at night by blue lights. It is hard to imagine any circumstance, outside of a health emergency, when one would actually need to use one of those—but they are there just the same. In short, you need not worry about crime or personal safety on the Pepperdine campus. You may worry, however, about the rather hazard-prone roadways nearby, such as Pacific Coast Highway and the perilous Malibu Canyon Road. The fact that going anywhere requires traversing one of these roads makes designated drivers all the more essential to any late-night partying, especially since Pepperdine's bone-dry campus forces partiers to drive elsewhere for their shenanigans.

A

The College Prowler® Grade on
Safety & Security: A

A high grade in Safety & Security means that students generally feel safe, campus police are visible, blue-light phones and escort services are readily available, and safety precautions are not overly necessary.

Computers

The Lowdown On...
Computers

High-Speed Network?
Yes

Wireless Network?
Yes

Number of Labs:
7, plus 6–12 technology-enabled classrooms (varies by semester)

Number of Computers:
Over 300 for general use, plus several hundred department-specific PCs

Operating Systems:
Windows
Mac OS

24-hour Labs?
In the Howard A. White Center (HAWC)

Free Software

FrontPage, Microsoft Office (for Windows and Mac), Publisher, Windows XP Professional

Discounted Software

Microsoft Office: $10

Charge to Print?

Yes

Did You Know?

Wireless Internet is available in all public places on campus, meaning labs, classrooms, the cafeteria, and just about anywhere except for the dorms, which have the standard Ethernet connections.

Students Speak Out On...
Computers

"The school network can be a bit slow in dorm rooms, and school computer labs tend to be full. I would definitely bring a personal computer."

Q "The computer connection at Pepperdine is just excellent. **I've never used a better one**. While there are computer labs available, the computers offered are pretty clunky and old. There are some snazzy new ones in the student center, but they're mainly for Internet, and they don't offer printing services. I would recommend bringing your own computer if possible, though I know people who haven't had much trouble getting along without one. If you don't have a computer, I would suggest getting a portable USB disk drive."

Q "T3 is always nice, but **don't get caught up in downloading music—trust me**, you don't want to cross that bridge. For most of my time at Pepperdine, I considered my desktop to be my best friend. I don't know anyone who didn't have his or her own computer."

Q "Definitely bring your own computer. Laptops are the best, and the **wireless connection is readily available for nearby apartment-dwellers**."

Q "The Internet has always been very fast for me. I haven't visited the labs. My goodness, though—**yes, bring your own computer**."

Q "I brought my own computer, and I found that by the end of my time at Pepperdine, **I was predominantly using the campus computers**. In fact, by my senior year, I didn't even have the Internet hooked up to my computer, as the campus computers were quick and nearly always available."

Q "**If you bring a computer you'll be fine; if you don't, you'll be fine**. Either way, you'll be using campus computers sometime. They are very convenient."

Q "**Around finals and midterms, the computer labs are always very busy**. I found this to be motivating, though, when I was tired, overstressed, and overworked. Being around others helped keep me on track (otherwise, I would have fallen asleep)."

Q "I'd suggest that you bring your own computer. **The computer labs are unreliable**. You could lose papers pretty easily. Each room has high-speed Internet access, which is really convenient."

Q "Bring your own computer for convenience, but the **computer labs are always there when you need them**."

Q "**The computer labs are crowded**, but I've never seen it so crowded you couldn't find a computer to use. I'd bring one anyway, though."

Q "Bring your own computer. **You will need it**. A laptop is even better."

Q "Having your own computer in your room is the best, but if you cannot afford one, **there are plenty on campus**."

Q "**Computer labs can get crowded towards final and midterm time**. Most people have their own computer, and I find it to be the most convenient way to go. But, I do use the computer labs from time to time."

Q "**You should definitely bring your own computer**. You can work in the labs, but it's a pain. I strongly suggest you bring your own. I brought my laptop, and I live on it."

Q "Most people have their own computers. We have lots of labs; **just make sure you leave plenty of time to do a paper in a lab** in case it's full, which happens especially during finals."

The College Prowler Take On...
Computers

The consensus is that Pepperdine's computer labs are at least satisfactory for most students, although having a personal computer is more convenient. Interestingly, most students do use the labs at least once in a while, even if they have their own personal computers. More than a few students have found using the school's computers to be more expedient than doing their work at home on their PCs. Meanwhile, the Internet connection in the dorms provides enough speed and reliability to satisfy even the more technologically savvy students.

Yes, it is nice to have your own computer. Often, especially around midterms or finals, the computer lab can become deafening with obnoxious, procrastinating banter. And yes, having a laptop with wireless access is especially preferable, as it allows you to take advantage of the University's wireless network. But at Pepperdine you can almost always find an available computer to use, whether in the library, the Writing Center, or, if it's going to be an all-nighter, the 24-hour computer lab in the HAWC.

The College Prowler® Grade on

Computers: B

A high grade in Computers designates that computer labs are available, the computer network is easily accessible, and the campus' computing technology is up-to-date.

Facilities

The Lowdown On...
Facilities

Student Center:
The Howard A. White
Center, or the HAWC
(pronounced "Hawk")

The Sandbar

Athletic Center:
Firestone Fieldhouse
Ralphs-Straus Tennis Center

Libraries:
Payson Library

Campus Size:
830 acres

Popular Places to Chill:
The Caf

The grassy knolls around
the dorms

The HAWC

What Is There to Do on Campus?

For diversions between classes, Pepperdine's campus offers people-watching and coffee-drinking opportunities, and for the more athletically motivated, it has a pool, tennis courts, a gym, and a newly-improved weight room. Or, students can head to the HAWC student center for a game of pool or Ping-Pong.

Movie Theater on Campus?

No, although SGA provides a weekly free movie night in the Smothers Theatre.

Bar on Campus?

Are you kidding?

Coffeehouse on Campus?

Yes, the Coffee House, Islandz, and Café Fresca

Bowling on Campus?

No

Favorite Things to Do

Men's basketball games are somewhat popular, and student plays and musicals are usually a big hit, too (probably because, at such a small school, everyone on campus knows at least one of the starring thespians). For the most part, though, students are looking to get away from campus in the evenings, if they possibly can.

Students Speak Out On...
Facilities

{ **"The facilities are mostly nicely kept. The gym is great, as is the pool and hot tub. The student center suffers from the abuse of students, but it remains in decent shape."**

Q "**Our gym isn't anything too special**, but our sports teams aren't either, so it kind of fits."

Q "The HAWC student center was remodeled a couple years ago and looks beautiful. **It's a good place to hang out between classes**. A bunch of new computers were installed throughout campus at that time, but the ones available for student use are still pretty ancient. The HAWC has a coffee house and some recreation, like Ping-Pong, pool, and foosball. It's a really great place to go do homework if you get sick of being in your dorm room. A lot of people hang out there for group projects. It's definitely an excellent facility."

Q "**I think the facilities on campus are very nice**. All of the buildings are well maintained and attractive."

Q "**Definitely take advantage of the intramural aerobics** classes, because no one likes to gain the Freshman 15."

Q "I love the overall campus and the facilities. If you are into science, they recently built a **new 30,000-square-foot building called the Keck Science Center**. It's awesome."

Q "**The student center (HAWC) is nice**—maybe a little small—but Pepperdine is a small school."

Q "**The workout center is very, very small for a Division I school**, so be prepared for it to be crowded."

Q "**Everything but the athletic center is fabulous and glossy**. The gym and weight room are rat-infested, ready to fall down, unsafe, and without enough equipment. Join a gym if you're a gym-rat."

Q "The weight room is pretty good, the track just got redone, and the **computer facilities are top-notch**."

Q "The weight room is sadly small. The buildings are nice, but **after four years of stucco, you tend to crave some sort of architectural variation**. The HAWC and the Sandbar are very comfortable and usually filled with people to spend time with. The Sandbar looks like a spot from Chuck E. Cheese's, but it's all a matter of taste, right?"

Q "**The facilities are very nice** and pretty much new, for the most part. The gym is kind of small, but it is free. There is a pool and hot tub, too. The library is kind of small, but then there is also the Law Library on top of the hill."

Q "**The gym sucks**. Everything else is awesome."

Q "The facilities are all very good. The computer labs are great, and they keep up with the latest computer technology. The athletic facilities are all good. The weight room is a little on the small side, but they have all the appropriate equipment. **The track is kept in good condition, and the tennis courts are amazing**."

Q "The campus has nice, new facilities. It's a small school, so **you don't always have all the amenities of a big school**, but it's quaint, and the natural scenery is incredible. Pepperdine is on a hill that overlooks the gorgeous Pacific Ocean. You can't beat the view here."

The College Prowler Take On...
Facilities

Pepperdine's beautiful campus is maintained in such a way that everything is white, immaculate, and uniform at all times—no dingy bricks or dirty ivory in sight! And what the architecture lacks in diversity and history, it makes up for with singleness of purpose and a calming, sterilized unity. Students seem enthralled with the dorms, the computer labs, and most of the other facilities—although there is some disagreement regarding the quality of the workout amenities.

One area in which Pepperdine could still improve itself is its single undergraduate library. Technologically and ergonomically, it is an impressive little building. Why, to the naked eye, Payson Library houses as many computers as it does books! Therein lies the problem, however. Most of the relatively few books and journals Pepperdine does keep on hand are woefully outdated; the shelves seem filled with fragile, dusty tomes donated to the University 40 years ago by its more fragile and dusty alumni. Thus, students needing research materials are bound to find themselves commuting to UCLA's libraries, or else restricting their research to Pepperdine's online databases.

B+

The College Prowler® Grade on
Facilities: B+

A high Facilities grade indicates that the campus is aesthetically pleasing and well-maintained; facilities are state-of-the-art, and libraries are exceptional. Other determining factors include the quality of both athletic and student centers and an abundance of things to do on campus.

Campus Dining

The Lowdown On...
Campus Dining

Freshman Meal Plan Requirement?

Yes

Meal Plan Average Cost:

$3,000 per semester

Places to Grab a Bite with Your Meal Plan:

Café Fresca

Food: Sandwiches, salads, snacks, coffee

Location: Center for Communications and Business

Hours: Monday–Thursday
7 a.m.–8 p.m.,
Friday 7 a.m.–6:30 p.m.,
Saturday 9:30 a.m.–6:30 p.m.,
Sunday 9:30 a.m.–7 p.m.

Coffee Cart

Food: Coffee, pastries

Location: Outside
Tyler Campus Center, by
the fountain

Hours: Monday–Friday
7:30 a.m.–2 p.m.

The Coffee House

Food: Smoothies, cookies,
snacks, coffee, sandwiches,
salads

Location: The HAWC

Hours: Monday–Thursday
7:30 a.m.–12 a.m.,
Friday 7:30 a.m.–10 p.m.,
Saturday 10 a.m.–5 p.m.,
Sunday 12 p.m.–12 a.m.

Islandz

Food: Pastries, coffee

Location: The Sandbar

Hours: Monday–Sunday
4:30 p.m.–11:30 p.m.

Oasis

Food: Pizza, fresh
sandwiches, smoothies

Location: Rockwell
Dining Center

Hours: Sunday–Friday
10:30 a.m.–10:30 p.m.,
Saturday 10:30 a.m.–5 p.m.

TAC Dining Room

Food: Continental breakfast
and a hot buffet lunch,
augmented by pre-packaged
sandwiches and salads

Location: Thorton
Administrative Center (TAC)

Hours: Monday–Friday
7:30 a.m.–2 p.m.

The Waves Café

Food: Salad bar, fresh entrée
stations, soups, desserts

Location: Rockwell
Dining Center

Hours: Monday–Thursday
7 a.m.–8 p.m.,
Friday 7 a.m.–6:30 p.m.,
Saturday 9:30 a.m.–6:30 p.m.,
Sunday 9:30 a.m.–7 p.m.

Off-Campus Places to Use Your Meal Plan:

None, although the University
has claimed for the last few
years that someday students
will be able to use their ID
cards to purchase groceries
at Ralphs and meals at
local restaurants.

24-Hour On-Campus Eating?

No

Student Favorites

For breakfast, students love to make fresh waffles on the griddles provided in the Waves Café, or to order fresh omelets just the way they like 'em. From lunchtime on, you'll find a steady line of people at TAC Dining Hall for burgers and fries, and at the Oasis for pizza and sandwiches.

Did You Know?

Now, **students can even have the Oasis deliver pipin' hot pizza** to the comfort of their on-campus suites or apartments!

Students Speak Out On...
Campus Dining

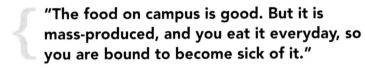

"The food on campus is good. But it is mass-produced, and you eat it everyday, so you are bound to become sick of it."

Q "There are very few choices for on-campus dining. The main one, where you will eat as an underclassman, is referred to as the 'Caf.' Compared to most dining halls in colleges around the country, the Caf is first-class. Different meal choices are offered at five or six different stations at once, and it's almost impossible not to find something you want to eat. **The food is fairly edible, but becomes less so once you figure out the rotation schedule** for the small range of meal choices available. Your best bet for consistently good food is the pizza, the grill, or the freshly-made deli sandwiches."

Q "**The Caf makes the best veggie burgers and fries I have ever tasted**. I never really ventured off campus, because I always had a bunch of points left over."

Q "Make friends with underclassmen, because you never know when **you'll find yourself with no points, and craving an ice-blended mocha** with soymilk and a shot of raspberry."

Q "There's only one arena for the eat-all, see-all experience: Waves. The food is great, and the staff is very helpful, but **there's a rumor that they dowse the leaf lettuce with starch to fatten up the would-be anorexics** that are so plentiful on campus."

Q "Food at Waves Café is not very good, except for the barbeque chicken salad. The desserts are fine, but everything else is very greasy. They tend to recycle the same meals every week. **It gets kind of boring**. The dining hall is spacious. There is a section right next to a fireplace that's cozy to eat and work at. It can get kind of loud, though, which makes the outside seating very nice."

Q "Food on campus gets old quick. It's okay, but not great. **There isn't much variety on campus—only one cafeteria**."

Q "The food is pretty good. The dining system is à la carte, unlike most schools. You use a point system for what you take, so you **can't go up again and again for more food**. At least it kind of keeps you from pigging out."

Q "The food is great in comparison to other college cafeteria food. **The food is cooked to order by several chefs**. Some people complain about the food, but I think it's because they want something to whine about."

Q "The food is great, compared to other schools. **Go anywhere else, and you'll complain**. Go to Pepperdine, and you'll be like, 'wow.'"

Q "**Points don't carry over to the next semester**, and some people have gripes about that."

Q "The food in the cafeteria is okay. It's better than most campuses, and you get more of a selection, but it closes at 8 p.m. **The law school is not far from the undergraduate school, and that has really good food**. The HAWC has a café with little things like muffins and cookies. That is your only source of food after 7 p.m."

Q "**No fast food! Thank heavens**. It is all catered, and we have a Seattle's Best Coffee, which is a great place to study and get much-needed coffee. It's located near the dorms, so it's easy to get to."

Q "The food on campus is all right. **You can eat only so many turkey sandwiches**—but the deli on campus is good enough, in my opinion."

Q "Campus food is awesome; **they actually served shark one night for dinner**. People complain about it, but I guess they haven't experienced bad dorm food."

Q "The food on campus is probably a lot better than what other schools' cafeterias have to offer, but that is still not saying a lot. **The Oasis always has good sammies, and Pepperdine does offer a very lovely dining hall**."

The College Prowler Take On...
Campus Dining

Few Pepperdine students seem to appreciate fully the fine culinary offerings heaped onto their plates by the good people at Sodexho Marriott Services. This could mean one of two things: either a select few of us have very low standards, or the Pepperdine student body has extraordinarily high ones. Still, it's certainly safe to say that Pepperdine can number itself among the better-tasting American universities. The basic meal plan is more than sufficient, even for those who just can't resist getting double heaping portions of the ever-reliable London Broil, or succulent pork tenderloin sliced right before their eyes by the steady hands of the Waves Café personnel. Don't worry, there are also plenty of vegetarian offerings. The "Caf," as students always call it, is the main dining area on campus, and it features many very large windows through which to gaze at the blue Pacific while you chomp your way through a delectable meal. Some might express displeasure regarding the dearth of dining halls, but the one Pepperdine does offer leaves little to complain about.

Just around the corner from the Caf, the Oasis serves pizza and made-to-order sandwiches on fresh-baked bread. Most eating takes place at either the Caf or the Oasis, but the little coffee counters on campus offer pre-packaged sandwiches and salads that are really quite good, as far as pre-packaged sandwiches and salads go. On the downside, to eat exclusively at Pepperdine is not an inexpensive endeavor, and the 1,000-point standard meal plan expires at the end of each semester—whether or not you've exhausted all your points. In keeping with its Christian mission, however, Pepperdine does give students the option of donating those unused points toward food for the needy.

B+

The College Prowler® Grade on
Campus Dining: B+

Our grade on Campus Dining addresses the quality of both school-owned dining halls and independent on-campus restaurants, as well as the price, availability, and variety of food.

Off-Campus Dining

The Lowdown On...
Off-Campus Dining

Restaurant Prowler:
Popular Places to Eat!

Allegria

Food: Italian

22821 Pacific Coast Hwy., Malibu

(310) 456-3132

www.allegriamalibu.com

Cool Features: Just two miles south of campus, and the food is terrific.

Price: $12–$25

(Allegria, continued)

Hours: Monday–Sunday 11:30 a.m.–3 p.m., Monday–Friday 5 p.m.–10 p.m., Saturday–Sunday 3 p.m.–10 p.m.

Beau Rivage

Food: Mediterranean

26025 Pacific Coast Hwy., Malibu

(310) 456-5733

Cool Features: Right next to the water.

Price: $19–$37

Hours: Monday–Saturday 5 p.m.–11 p.m., Sunday 11 a.m.–11 p.m.

→

Chart House

Food: Seafood

18412 Pacific Coast
Hwy., Malibu

(310) 454-9321

Cool Features: Great views of
the Pacific and Santa Monica
Bay; right on Topanga Beach.

Price: $20–$25

Hours: Monday–Thursday
5 p.m.–9:30 p.m.,
bar opens at 4 p.m.,
Friday 5 p.m.–10 p.m.,
bar opens at 4 p.m.,
Saturday 11 a.m.–10 p.m.,
Sunday 11 a.m.–9:30 p.m.

China Den

Food: Chinese

22333 Pacific Coast
Hwy., Malibu

(310) 456-8541

Cool Features: Great sushi and
lunch specials.

Price: $10–$15

Hours: Monday–Saturday
11 a.m.–10 p.m.,
Sunday 3 p.m.–10 p.m.

Cheesecake Factory

Food: American

442 West Hillcrest Dr.,
Thousand Oaks

(805) 371-9705

Cool Features: As famous for
its heaping portions as it is for
its cheesecake.

Price: $10–$15 per person

Hours: Sunday–Thursday
11 a.m.–12 a.m.,
Friday–Saturday
11 a.m.–1 a.m.

Coogie's Beach Café

Food: Sandwiches, salads

23755 W. Malibu Rd., Malibu

(310) 317-1444

Cool Features: Look for movie
stars while you eat, and then
go next door for dessert at
Malibu Yogurt.

Price: $13–$20

Hours: Sunday–Thursday
7:30 a.m.–9 p.m.,
Friday–Saturday
7:30 a.m.–9:30 p.m.

Duke's Malibu

Food: Burgers, seafood

21150 Pacific Coast
Hwy., Malibu

(310) 317-0777

www.dukesmalibu.com

Cool Features: Longest
beach-facing bar on the West
Coast, has surfer memorabilia
displaying its homage to Duke
Kahanamoku and to other
surfers.

Price: $15–$25

Hours: Monday 5–9 p.m.,
Tuesday–Thursday
11 a.m.–3 p.m.,5 p.m.–9 p.m.,
Friday 5 p.m.–9 p.m.,
Saturday 4:30 p.m.–10 p.m.,
Sunday 10 a.m.–9 p.m.

Geoffrey's

Food: Steak and seafood

27400 Pacific Coast
Hwy., Malibu

(310) 457-1519

www.geoffreysmalibu.com

Cool Features: Plenty of
outdoor dining, right by

(Geoffrey's, continued)

the ocean.

Price: Brunch/lunch $14–$24, dinner $20–$45

Hours: Monday–Thursday 11:30 a.m.–10 p.m., Friday 11:30 a.m.–11 p.m., Saturday 10 a.m.–11 p.m., Sunday 10 a.m.–10 p.m.

Gladstone's 4 Fish

Food: Seafood, enormous desserts

17300 Pacific Coast Hwy., Malibu

(310) 454-3574

Cool Features: Ocean view, shares parking with public beach

Price: $20–$45

Hours: Monday–Thursday 11 a.m.–11 p.m., Friday 11 a.m.–12 p.m., Saturday 7 a.m.–12 a.m., Sunday 7 a.m.–11 p.m.

The Gray Whale

Food: Pasta, seafood, steaks

6800 Westward Beach Rd., Malibu

(310) 457-5521

Cool Features: It's located right on Zuma Beach.

Price: $14–$22

Hours: Sunday–Thursday 5 p.m.–10 p.m., Friday–Saturday 5 p.m.–11 p.m.

Guido's

Food: Italian

3874 Crosscreek Rd., Malibu

(310) 456-1979 or (800) 4-GUIDOS

Cool Features: Popular celebrity place.

Price: Lunch $8–$15, dinner $12–$30

Hours: Monday–Thursday 11:30 a.m.–2:30 p.m., 5 p.m.–10 p.m., Friday 11:30 a.m.–2:30 p.m., 5 p.m.–10:30 p.m., Saturday 5 p.m.–10:30 p.m., Sunday 4 p.m.–10 p.m.

Howdy's Taqueria

Food: Mexican

3835 Crosscreek Rd., Malibu

(310) 456-6299

Cool Features: Try the breakfast burrito and the "Pepperdine Burrito."

Price: $4–$7

Hours: Daily 9 a.m.–5 p.m.

Jack in the Box

Food: Fast food

23017 Pacific Coast Hwy., Malibu

(310) 456-8943

Cool Features: Two tacos for $.99 at 4 a.m.—can't beat it!

Price: $4–$10

Hours: Daily 24 hours

Johnnie's New York Pizzeria

Food: Pizza, pastas, sandwiches

22333 Pacific Coast Hwy., Malibu

(310) 456-1717

Cool Features: Delicious New York-style pizza.

Price: $8–$22

Hours: Sunday–Thursday 11 a.m.–10 p.m., Friday–Saturday 11 a.m.–11 p.m.

La Paz

Food: Mexican

4505 Las Virgenes Rd., Calabasas

(818) 880-8076

Cool Features: Donate dollar bills to charity by shooting them up onto the ceiling with a rubber band. The waiter will put a thumbtack in the bill first so that it sticks.

Price: $10–$20

Hours: Monday–Thursday 11 a.m.–9 p.m., Friday–Saturday 11 a.m.–10 p.m., Sunday 10 a.m.–2 p.m., 2:30 p.m.–9 p.m.

La Salsa

Food: Mexican

22800 Pacific Coast Hwy., Malibu

(310) 317-9466

Cool Features: The big guy in a sombrero standing on the roof is a Malibu landmark.

(La Salsa continued)

Price: $4–$7

Hours: Daily 8 a.m.–9 p.m.

Malibu Seafood

Food: Seafood

25653 Pacific Coast Hwy., Malibu

(310) 456-3430 or (310) 456-6298

Cool Features: The fish 'n chips is out of this world.

Price: $5–$15

Hours: Daily 1 a.m.–7 p.m. during the winter, Daily 11 a.m.–9 p.m. in the summer

Marmalade Café

Food: American

3894 Crosscreek Rd., Malibu

(310) 317-4242

Cool Features: For lunch, get the Monte Cristo sandwich.

Price: $15–$25

Hours: Sunday–Thursday 7:30 a.m.–9 p.m., Friday–Saturday 7:30 a.m.–10 p.m.

Moonshadows

Food: Seafood

20356 Pacific Coast Hwy., Malibu

(310) 456-3010

Cool Features: On the beach with a tiki bar.

Price: $18–$40

(Moonshadows continued)

Hours: Monday–Sunday
11 a.m.–4 p.m., Sunday–
Thursday 4 p.m.–10:30 p.m.,
Friday–Sunday 4 p.m.–
11 p.m., Brunch: Saturday–
Sunday 11 a.m.–3 p.m.

Neptune's Net

Food: Seafood

42505 Pacific Coast
Hwy., Malibu

(310) 457-3095

www.neptunesnet.com

Cool Features: Regulars call it
"the Net."

Price: $13–$26

Hours: Monday–Thursday
10 a.m.–8 p.m.,
Friday 11:30 a.m.–9 p.m.,
Saturday–Sunday
10 a.m.–8:30 p.m.

Nobu

Food: Sushi

3835 Crosscreek Rd., Malibu

(310) 317-9140 or
(310) 317-9137

Cool Features: The staff shouts
a welcome as customers enter.

Price: $15–$25

Hours: Sunday–Thursday
5:45 p.m.–10 p.m.,
Friday–Saturday
5:45 p.m.–11 p.m.

Paradise Cove Beach Café

Food: Seafood

28128 Pacific Coast
Hwy., Malibu

(310) 457-9791

Cool Features: Free beach
parking at Paradise Cove if you
eat in the restaurant.

Price: $15–$20

Hours: Monday–Friday
8 a.m.–10 p.m.,
Saturday–Sunday
7 a.m.–10 p.m.

Reel Inn

Food: Seafood

18661 Pacific Coast
Hwy., Malibu

(310) 456-8221

Cool Features: Cheap beach
dining, fresh seafood.

Price: $8–$16

Hours: Daily 11 a.m.–10 p.m.

Sage Room

Food: Mediterranean

28915 Pacific Coast
Hwy., Malibu

(310) 457-0711

Cool Features: Authentic Italian
food, great ambiance, and
exceptional wine list.

Price: $10–$30

Hours: Monday–Saturday
5 p.m.–10 p.m.,
Sunday 10:30 a.m.–3 p.m.,
5 p.m.–10 p.m.

Spruzzo's

Food: Pizza, steaks, pasta

29575 Pacific Coast
Hwy., Malibu

(310) 457-8282

Cool Features: Three dining
areas, "each with its own
distinctive sensory stimulus."

Price: $10–$20

Hours: Sunday–Thursday
11:30 a.m.–9 p.m.,
Friday–Saturday
11:30 a.m.–10 p.m.

Taverna Tony

Food: Greek

23410 Civic Center
Way, Malibu

(310) 317-9667

Cool Features: House
bouzouki band.

Price: $15–$30

Hours: Sunday–Thursday
11:30 a.m.–12 a.m.,
Friday–Saturday
11:30 a.m.–12:30 a.m.

Thai Dishes

Food: Thai

22333 Pacific Coast
Hwy., Malibu

(310) 456-6592

Cool Features: Karaoke and
sake bombing.

Price: $12–$20

Hours: Daily
11 a.m.–10:30 p.m.

Tra Di Noi

Food: Italian

3835 Crosscreek Rd., Malibu

(310) 456-0169

Cool Features: Just two
miles from campus, another
celebrity hotspot.

Price: $15–$25

Hours: Daily 12 p.m.–10 p.m.

Tutto Bene

Food: Italian

22235 Pacific Coast
Hwy., Malibu

(310) 317-6769

Cool Features: Many celebs
frequent this restaurant.

Price: $12–$28

Hours: Daily 5 p.m.–10 p.m.

Wood Ranch

Food: Barbecue

5050 Cornell Rd., Agoura Hills

(818) 597-8900

Cool Features: Authentic
Texas-style barbecue,
delicious tri-tips.

Price: $12–$30

Hours: Monday–Thursday
4 p.m.–10 p.m.,
Friday 4 p.m.–11 p.m.,
Saturday 3 p.m.–11 p.m.,
Sunday 2 p.m.–10 p.m.

Zooma Sushi

Food: Sushi, teriyaki, tempura

29350 Pacific Coast Hwy., Malibu

(310) 317-0127

www.zoomasushi.net

Cool Features: Best sushi in Malibu since 1987. Early bird specials; reservations recommended.

Price: $13–$17

Hours: Sunday–Thursday 5 p.m.–10 p.m., Friday–Saturday 5 p.m.–10:30 p.m.

24-Hour Eating:

Jack in the Box

Best Pizza:

Johnnie's New York Pizzeria

Best Chinese:

China Den

Best Breakfast:

Coogie's Beach Café

Best Wings:

Duke's Malibu

Best Healthy:

Nobu

Best Place to Take Your Parents:

Nobu

Closest Grocery Stores:

Ralphs

Sav-on

Student Favorites:

Duke's

Howdy's Taqueria

Marmalade Café

Other Places to Check Out:

BJ's

Houston's

Kentucky Fried Chicken

McDonald's

Pier View

Subway

Students Speak Out On...
Off-Campus Dining

"Most restaurants are expensive, but there are a few reasonable spots. Malibu is small, so just go to the ones that don't look like they're really expensive."

Q "**Restaurants are few and far between**, due to Malibu being such a small town."

Q "As Malibu is an intensely small town, the number of student-affordable restaurants off campus is pretty small. Malibu residents oppose letting chains into the area, so there aren't many of those around. Besides basic fast food (McDonald's, Jack in the Box, Subway) there are a couple excellent fresh-Mex places (La Salsa, Howdy's). **The main disappointment is the lack of a reputable pizza chain that delivers on campus**."

Q "**One moderately-priced restaurant I always take my family to is Coogies**. It's five minutes from campus, the food is great, and the chances are pretty good that you'll see somebody famous there."

Q "If you are willing to trek through the canyon (20 to 30 minutes) or down the Pacific Coast Highway (20 minutes), **there are a huge number of excellent restaurants available to you in the LA area**. Some of the great ones, if you are willing to spend a little more, include Allegria, Moonshadows, Gladstone's 4 Fish, and Houston's."

Q "**Malibu is overpriced**. No matter what anyone else says, the fare at Howdy's just tastes like normal food. There really is nothing special about it."

Q "It's LA, so we have some of the best places to eat and drink in the country. **Malibu can get pricey**, but there's always the Valley for a delicious, well-priced meal at BJ's. Mmm."

Q "**Don't be a stranger to Duke's** Monday through Friday from 4 p.m. to 7 p.m., when everything in the Barefoot Bar is half off."

Q "**Restaurants off campus are not bad**. Check out Duke's Malibu."

Q "The restaurants in Malibu are absolutely phenomenal! **Howdy's is the best Mexican food**. It is real Mexican food, not wannabe Mexican food. I also love Neptune's Net."

Q "**There are lots of restaurants—we're near LA**! Some good restaurants are Duke's, Marmalade, Coogie's . . . the list goes on and on."

Q "**There are a good handful of restaurants around campus, and some very expensive ones, too**. Coogie's and Marmalade are both popular."

Q "Off campus, the restaurants are great not only in Malibu, but **Santa Monica and Venice as well**. There are great places to eat in the surrounding area."

Q "Off campus you can get Jack In The Box or eat from **world famous chefs like Wolfgang Puck** and Nobu."

The College Prowler Take On...
Off-Campus Dining

To cater to the rich but laid-back local population, restaurants all along the Malibu coast represent a mix of gourmet cooking, overpriced novelties, and fun little places to get a sandwich or some seafood at somewhat reasonable prices. Of course, the old standbys receive most of the attention and lunch money of Pepperdine students. It's nearly impossible to walk into Coogie's, La Salsa, or Howdy's without seeing someone you know. The food at these and other places is reliably delicious and affordable, and their popularity among the student body makes for an off-campus community atmosphere not to be found elsewhere.

As for the more expensive Malibu restaurants, students on any sort of a budget obviously can't afford to partake very often. When someone mentions that his or her parents came last weekend to visit, the first question to pop out of other students' mouths is where did they take you to eat? The next question will likely be which celebrities did you see there? The downside to off-campus dining is that you virtually have to be a movie star or a hit recording artist to afford some of the great Malibu offerings on a regular basis. The variety of cheaper options, other than those mentioned above, is not overwhelming.

B-

The College Prowler® Grade on
Off-Campus
Dining: B-

A high Off-Campus Dining grade implies that off-campus restaurants are affordable, accessible, and worth visiting. Other factors include the variety of cuisine and the availability of alternative options (vegetarian, vegan, Kosher, etc.).

Campus Housing

The Lowdown On...
Campus Housing

Undergrads Living on Campus:
62%

Number of Dormitories:
4

Best Dorms:
Honors Apartments

Worst Dorms:
Greek Row in the Suites
Residence Halls

→

Dormitories:

Honors Apartments

Floors: Three

Total Occupancy: 200 (not counting grad students)

Bathrooms: 1 per four single bedrooms

Coed: Yes

Residents: Upperclassmen

Room Type: Single

Special Features: Students get access to outdoor barbecues, a fitness center, and a covered parking garage. Best of all, they have no roommates.

Lovernich Residential Complex

Buildings: 3

Total Occupancy: 300

Bathrooms: 1 per two-bedroom apartment

Coed: Yes

Residents: Upperclassmen

Room Type: Double

Special Features: Each apartment has its own kitchenette.

Rockwell Towers

Floors: 4 with 6 wings

Total Occupancy: 275

Bathrooms: 1 per four-person suite

Coed: Guys get wings 1–2, girls get wings 3–6.

Residents: Upperclassmen

(Rockwell Towers, continued)

Room Type: Double

Special Features: The main lounge has a big-screen TV and a kitchenette.

Suite Residence Halls

Buildings: 22

Total Occupancy: 50 per building (1,100 total)

Bathrooms: 1 double per eight-person suite

Coed: Yes, by building

Residents: Roughly 82 percent are freshmen, and the rest primarily sophomores

Room Type: Double (two students, two beds, two desks, two dressers, and two small bookcases).

Special Features: Aside from the living area in each suite, each dorm has a large lobby with a fireplace and TV.

Housing Offered:

Singles: 6%

Doubles: 78%

Triples/Suites: 1%

Apartments: 15%

Room Types

All freshmen must live on campus in the Suite Residence Halls. Each of these 22 dorms is designated all-boys or all-girls and offers comfortable living, sizeable rooms, and usually an excellent view. After freshman year, students can apply to live in these same dorms or up the hill in the Rockwell Towers (basically mini-suites for four people, with two bedrooms and access to a community kitchenette). For juniors and seniors, there is the Lovernich Residential Complex (similar to the Towers, but with a kitchen in every four-person apartment). Best of all, though, are the Honors Apartments, which feature four small single bedrooms per apartment—no roommates— as well as a kitchen and sizeable living area. The Housing Office gives priority to students with at least a 3.0 GPA, so keep those grades up if you want your own room on campus.

Bed Type

Twin, extra-long

Available for Rent

Mini-fridge with microwave oven, Sparkletts water cooler

Cleaning Service?

Janitors clean the living areas and bathrooms daily.

What You Get

Bed, cable TV jack, desk and chair, dresser, Ethernet connection, free local and campus calls, and a hanging closet

Did You Know?

The term "Greek Row," does not have anything to do with fraternities or sororities. The **Greeks have no on-campus houses**. Greek Row is the residence halls farthest from the central campus. Unlike the closer dorms, which are numbered, these dorms have Greek letters for names.

Students Speak Out On...
Campus Housing

"The dorms, I must admit, are incredibly snazzy. I've never seen dorms at another college to match them, and they played a big role in my decision to come to Pepperdine."

"All of the freshman dorms are technically equal, but if you are in one close to the HAWC and main campus, you're lucky. Greek Row dorms, as they're nicknamed, are a little bit of a trek, but if you're lazy, you can always take the shuttle to main campus. After your freshman year, the apartments are your best bet for on-campus housing. The only other option available is Towers, which is pretty isolated and private. **The nicest places on campus are the Honors Apartments**, with four single rooms. They cost a little more, but are just gorgeous if you can afford it. They have the best views on campus, which is saying something."

"**From a girl who had massive roommate problems, try to get a single room**. If you can't, keep an eye on your bananas, or your roommate will throw them away when you're not looking."

"Try and locate one near the buildings (closer to food and classes), **and get off campus as soon as you can**."

"**Dorms have been rated 'castles' before on a scale that goes down to the 'dungeons' levels**. They have finished, white walls, navy carpets, and a suite format. They come with one living room, four double bedrooms, and a bathroom. There are six suites in a house. There are no dorms to avoid; they're all the same. Most have amazing ocean views."

Q "All dorms are relatively nice at Pepperdine. **Just think tract housing.**"

Q "The dorms are very nice for college living. The suite situation is very helpful, because **you get to meet several people in your first year**, as opposed to just your roommate. Try avoiding dorms that are in Greek Row. They are very far away from campus! As far as facilities go, though, they are all the same."

Q "**The dorms are kind of crappy**. I got an ocean-view room, so I have nothing to complain about."

Q "Avoid being placed in the back dorms. **The walk to class is at least a half-mile.**"

Q "In comparison to other schools, the dorms are like palaces—but they are still dorms. **You want a dorm close to the center of campus**. The Greek dorms, as they are called, are quite a walk."

Q "The dorms are some of the biggest that I've ever seen. They are large, and a **majority of them overlook the ocean**. There are suites that have two toilets, two sinks, and two showers for eight people, which isn't too bad. They are very nice dorms."

Q "There are no coed dorms until you get into the Towers, which are where graduate students and upperclassmen get to live. No boys are allowed in your room after midnight or in your dorm after one in the morning. **Some people there are really strict with the rules—I'm talking students**—so they might narc on you and get you kicked out."

The College Prowler Take On...
Campus Housing

You know the campus housing is pretty impressive when such an affluent student body as Pepperdine's tends to lob terms like "palace" and "castle" around to describe it. Indeed, freshman dorms well reflect the University's eagerness to ensconce its students in comfort and splendor. Folks expecting dingy halls stacked in tall, shabby buildings will likely be taken aback by the well-lit and freshly-painted opulence that awaits them. Freshmen luxuriate in suites of four bedrooms (two students to a room), a large double bathroom, and a pleasant living area replete with television and a picture window offering Pepperdine's most treasured asset, the ocean view. Friendly janitors clean the bathrooms and living areas daily.

This living arrangement offers certain benefits, but also a few shortcomings. Freshmen get to know their seven suitemates very well (maybe a little too well for many people's liking), and friendships form quickly within the suites. On the other hand, students can settle too comfortably into these relationships and not get to know as many other people in their dorms, as kids in a more traditional residence hall might. Also, the dorms' restrictive policies can grate on students who aren't used to random "room checks" or to being told when they can and cannot fraternize with members of the opposite sex. Nevertheless, one has to admit that Pepperdine's student housing is pretty darn nice.

The College Prowler® Grade on

Campus Housing: A

A high Campus Housing grade indicates that dorms are clean, well-maintained, and spacious. Other determining factors include variety of dorms, proximity to classes, and social atmosphere.

Off-Campus Housing

The Lowdown On...
Off-Campus Housing

Undergrads in Off-Campus Housing:

38%

Average Rent For:

1BR Apt.: $1,000/month

2BR Apt.: $1,200/month

3BR Apt.: $1,500/month

Popular Areas:

Agoura Hills, Calabasas, Malibu, Westlake, Woodland Hills

For Assistance Contact:

www.pepperdine.edu/housing/offcampus

(310) 506-4104

RLO@pepperdine.edu

Best Time to Look For a Place:

Beginning of second semester

Students Speak Out On...
Off-Campus Housing

"Expensive. Not worth it. Also, dangerous if you go over to the cheap end—on the other side of the canyon—because you have to drive through this mountainous area where people get into fatal car accidents too often."

"Moving off campus is worth it, but it is not very convenient. The most affordable apartments are through Malibu Canyon, a 15-minute drive on a narrow, dangerous road—making drinking and driving even more dangerous than it already is. Or, you can find an apartment in Malibu, but **the cost is going to be as ridiculous as the tuition**."

"While there are a few options for off-campus housing, **none of them are all that convenient**. It's actually kind of a hassle to be a commuter student, but the benefits lie in not having to live under Pepperdine's fairly strict dorm rules."

"Definitely try to live off campus, **because off campus means no dorm rules**."

"Off-campus housing is as convenient as you can make it, depending on where you choose to live. **Living in Malibu or Pacific Palisades is extremely convenient**, but very expensive. Most students choose to live through the canyon in Calabasas or Woodland Hills. These places are also very nice but not nearly as pretty as living near the ocean."

Q "**You have to move about 15 minutes away**; there are fewer rules, but it is less convenient."

Q "**You have the rest of your life to live off campus**. Enjoy the time you have on campus—you'll be more plugged into campus life."

Q "Though living off campus may not necessarily be as convenient as living on campus, it is very much worth it. **I didn't do it until my senior year, and I regret that**. You have your own space, away from the hustle of campus. You can have your own social gatherings, with your choice of alcoholic beverages, without having to worry about Public Safety releasing the dogs on you."

Q "**Housing is expensive**, but so is living in the dorms."

Q "Living in Malibu is very expensive; at least $1,000 per month for only an average, one-bedroom apartment. Many students decide to live in Calabasas, which is through the canyon. **Expect a 15- to 30-minute drive**. But you will find nice apartments for $1,000 to $1,300 for a one-bedroom, and $1,250 to $1,500 for a two-bedroom."

Q "It's fine. **I have many friends who lived off campus**."

Q "It's really expensive, and if you decide to move off campus, **it is a good idea to reserve a space the year before** because they always have a waiting list."

The College Prowler Take On...
Off-Campus Housing

Pepperdiners clearly find off-campus housing to be something of a hassle. If your wallet or purse isn't bursting with excess currency, living in Malibu is probably not an option. If you live "through the canyon," as most opt to do, prices are still fairly high, and the commute gets to be a pain in the neck (especially when they're doing road construction, which seems to be always, or when one slow driver clogs the entirety of Malibu Canyon and stretches your 11-mile trip into a half-hour journey). The consensus among many, though, is that it's worthwhile to put up with these little hassles if it means getting away from the watchful eye of Public Safety and the general tedium of campus living.

Of course, others point out that staying on campus will keep you better connected to your school. The campus cleaning service and lack of commute may be difficult luxuries to give up after you've grown accustomed to them. Yet most students do move off campus, despite issues of cost, commute, and inconvenience, and those who have moved off are usually glad they did.

The College Prowler® Grade on

Off-Campus Housing: C

A high grade in Off-Campus Housing indicates that apartments are of high quality, close to campus, affordable, and easy to secure.

Diversity

The Lowdown On...
Diversity

Native American:
2%

White:
60%

Asian American:
11%

International:
6%

African American:
8%

Out-of-State:
50%

Hispanic:
13%

Political Activity

Pepperdine's political atmosphere falls somewhere between quietly conservative and blissfully apolitical. Neither the College Republicans, nor the Young Democrats, manage to maintain much of a membership base, although the Young Democrats are especially unpopular. When voices are raised, they are usually either to defend or oppose Pepperdine's traditional Christian conservatism on matters such as homosexuality and women's roles in the church.

Gay Pride

People often think of college as a time and place for new ideas, liberal thought, and social acceptance. You can find these things at Pepperdine, but don't expect them to run rampant. Yes, most Pepperdine students are probably open-minded and accepting with regard to gays and lesbians, and there is even an awkwardly-titled club, the Gay and Lesbian-Straight Alliance, that promotes goodwill between people of different sexual orientations. But an atmosphere of homophobia definitely flourishes, despite the supposedly high percentage of gay men on campus.

Economic Status

The stereotypical Pepperdine student drives a BMW or a Porsche and never wears the same pair of designer jeans or high heels twice. However, people exaggerate the wealth and beauty of the Pepperdine student body because, even though many students are not rich or gorgeous, one tends to notice the dazzling blonde stepping out of a new Mercedes convertible, and not the backdrop of regular-looking and scholarship-funded college kids. Still, if you're looking for a preponderance of affluent students, look no further than Pepperdine.

Sample Minority Clubs

African Alliance, Armenian Student Association, Asian Student Association, the Black Student Union, Cultural Italian American Organization, Hawaii Club, Latino Student Association, Pepperdine International Club, Pepperdine University Hispanic Council

Students Speak Out On...
Diversity

{ **"The only ethnic variety on this campus is on the sports teams. Sounds sad, but it's the honest truth. A very small portion of the students are not white."**

Q "**There is a good foreign exchange program**, making the school comfortably diverse."

Q "**The campus, sad to say, is not very diverse**. We do have a fairly large contingent of really wealthy international students, but in terms of American minorities, the numbers are fairly small. I've heard that it's sometimes difficult to deal with the very conservative atmosphere of the campus as a whole."

Q "How diverse is campus? **Not very**."

Q "I'm Asian, and I found the campus to be more diverse than I originally thought. **It's a pretty fair mix of people**. I came from a mainly white neighborhood, so what one person would define as diverse might be something totally opposite than my definition. But, it's nice seeing people of different cultures around; it's definitely a good thing."

Q "Honestly, it could be more diverse, but even since my freshman year three years ago, **I feel like it has improved**. So it seems to be on the rise."

Q "**It's not diverse at all**. There are definitely far fewer minorities and international students than Caucasian students."

Q "There are lots of white kids, some rich Asians, and some Europeans. I'm Indian. **For the most part, the only black kids are on the basketball team**."

Q "**People think it's diverse; I think they're crazy**. It's pretty much Caucasian."

Q "The Pep population is pretty homogenous—all white kids. All the black kids, it seems, are on the basketball team. There are lots of international students, but these international students are either from Asia or Europe. I am Filipina and black. My friends are Hawaiian, white, and Mexican, and they all come from different socioeconomic backgrounds. Diversity does exist on this campus. **It just takes digging a little deeper to get to know people**."

Q "**Not at all diverse**. The African American men populate the basketball team."

Q "Pepperdine is **fairly diverse**, but it is not the extreme."

Q "**It depends on what you're used to**. I don't find it extremely diverse, but my roommate, who is from Arkansas, thinks it's very diverse."

The College Prowler Take On...
Diversity

Some are willing to give Pepperdine credit for trying, with its international exchange program and so on, but mostly students agree that diversity is not a Pepperdine hallmark. There are noticeably few black students, although to say, as many do, that the African American student population is limited strictly to the basketball team is probably to overstate Pepperdine's diversity deficiency. And gender-wise, both sexes are pretty prevalent on campus.

In all seriousness, though, diversity is a real problem in the sense that college applicants looking for a place to branch out culturally after high school will find Pepperdine disappointing. White Californians clearly dominate the campus scene; behind them there seems to be a glut of white folks from Colorado, Texas, and the Pacific Northwest. Not that there's anything wrong with white folks, or any of these fine locales, but Pepperdine could certainly use more ethnic and cultural variety.

The College Prowler® Grade on
Diversity: C

A high grade in Diversity indicates that ethnic minorities and international students have a notable presence on campus and that students of different economic backgrounds, religious beliefs, and sexual preferences are well-represented.

Guys & Girls

The Lowdown On...
Guys & Girls

Men Undergrads:
43%

Women Undergrads:
57%

Birth Control Available?

The Health Center personnel can prescribe birth control pills. They used to sell condoms as well, but Pepperdine's board of directors decided such behavior conflicted with the school's Christian mission.

Most Prevalent STDs on Campus

Herpes, HPV, and Chlamydia

Social Scene

Most students readily describe the dating scene at Pepperdine as bleak, if not nonexistent. Some say the hotness of the girls intimidates the guys; others say the established non-dating atmosphere itself precludes dating. Actually, though, more dating takes place among the more conservative (non-drinking, sexually inactive) students than meets the eye, while the wilder set seems content to hook up at parties.

Hookups or Relationships?

A little bit of both. Female students often cite Pepperdine as a good place to meet a prospective husband, (there's a perfect wedding chapel right on campus!). When people do date, it's usually in the context of a committed relationship. Hookups are not exactly rare, but girls tend to tread more carefully around such encounters than they might at a larger university because of the notorious "Peppervine" that makes the average high school rumor mill seem merciful and discreet.

Best Place to Meet Guys/Girls

In the cafeteria or the HAWC.

Dress Code

Girls: Whether you're headed to a sorority mixer, a prayer meeting, or an 8 a.m. class—come rain or shine—don't forget your short skirt, heels, fancy purse, makeup, and eye glitter.

Guys: Go for surfer casual, spendy-trendy casual (in which case you'll need a $50 mesh "trucker hat"), or go metro chic.

Did You Know?

Top Places to Find Hotties:

1. Lounging by the fountain

2. Lounging at the beach

3. Lounging on the dorm lawns

Top Places to Hook Up:

1. Bars

2. Frat parties

3. Other off-campus parties

4. Honors Apartments

5. UCLA

Students Speak Out On...
Guys & Girls

"I think that no Pepperdine student will disagree with me when I say that a person would be hard put to find a college campus with a higher percentage of absolutely gorgeous people. It's like being in a movie sometimes."

Q "**The dating scene is awful**. There aren't nearly enough guys for girls, and the guys aren't always dating material. They're better as friends."

Q "Guys are cookie-cutter, Abercrombie-wearing surfers. **Once in a while, you get your attractive, pensive, introspective bloke who loves literature**. He is usually already dating someone. The girls have blonde hair, tanned skin, and carry around Louis Vuitton handbags. There is a small population of hippie-type alternative men and women. But if you were an outsider looking in, you'd think the campus was made of all model-type men and women (a sort of Stepford University)."

Q "It's one of the greatest schools for people watching. I consider myself to be an eight on a scale from one to ten. **But, the school has tons of eights, nines, and tens—both male and female**."

Q "We're hot. Lots of mama's boys here, and little girls with their daddy's credit cards. But, **the pickings are good**. There's a high ratio of girls to boys; my boyfriend actually chose this school with that statistic in mind."

Q "**Think of the movie *Clueless* or *Mean Girls***. And there you have the population of Pepperdine."

Q "With a large portion of the school being both good-looking and rich, the Pepperdine campus is strangely reminiscent of a fashion show. This being said, **the dating scene is practically nonexistent**, unless you're looking to find a spouse or a short-term hookup."

Q "Guys and girls are varied. But I'd say that, overall, people are a lot nicer at Pepperdine, since it's not overly big, and most people have strong religious affiliations. **The girls are very hot**!"

Q "We have **nice-looking white people**."

Q "**I dare you to find an ugly person on the campus**. Pepperdine attracts beautiful people."

Q "Girls—oh yeah, **totally hot**! Guys, not my area."

Q "The guys are nice. I guess one could consider them hot. They are very nice. They are the surfer type, and so are the girls. **Guys and girls alike are very conscious of what they look like**."

Q "I've only been at Pep a semester, but the dating situation seems pretty pathetic to me. People either have been dating forever, or **the guys won't even ask girls out on a date**. It's really weird. There are lots of cute guys, but I think they're overwhelmed by the massive amount of attractive girls."

Q "**Be careful of the basketball players**. They are great guys, but girls get reputations really quickly by messing around with them."

Q "Pepperdine is a beautiful campus in all aspects. The girls here are gorgeous, as are the guys, but **most of the guys are gay**! Plus, the girl-to-guy ratio is uneven and unfair for me, as a girl. There are some great guys and awesome girls here, though."

Q "**People-wise, we were voted one of the most beautiful in the country, if not the most beautiful**. Our girls have been in *YM* and *Playboy*, and some are actresses. We even have some Abercrombie models."

Q "Most of the guys and the girls are pretty nice, and the girls are very pretty. **Some of the guys can be cute, but be careful, because there are a lot of gay people**."

The College Prowler Take On...
Guys & Girls

Students appear united in their opinions on the "guys and girls" issue. To sum up the quotes, as well as the general opinion on campus: (a) the girls are hot, (b) so are the guys, but (c) a lot of them are gay, and (d) no one dates. Students tend to conform, in terms of style and personality, and walking around Pepperdine is a little like watching a movie or attending a fashion show. Tight clothing and high heels predominate, and accessories bearing the names of venerable fashion avatars are a mainstay. Not to be outdone, even male students tote their books around in Coach and Louis Vuitton bags. Incidentally, such metrosexual behavior, along with the conservative environment that discourages explicit references to one's preferences, makes it hard to tell who's gay and who's not. Regardless, most students maintain that the gay population at Pepperdine is extraordinarily high.

Good luck, dear reader, finding a more attractive campus than Pepperdine's undergraduate school, Seaver College. The girls are otherworldly, and the guys, well, most of them look pretty good, too. What's more, some of these young men and women have personalities and are even pleasant to talk to! For what more could one ask?

The College Prowler® Grade on Guys: A-

A high grade for Guys indicates that the male population on campus is attractive, smart, friendly, and engaging, and that the school has a decent ratio of guys to girls.

The College Prowler® Grade on Girls: A+

A high grade for Girls not only implies that the women on campus are attractive, smart, friendly, and engaging, but also that there is a fair ratio of girls to guys.

Athletics

The Lowdown On...
Athletics

Athletic Division:
NCAA Division I

Conference:
West Coast Conference

School Mascot:
Waves

**Males Playing
Varsity Sports:**
113 (10%)

**Females Playing
Varsity Sports:**
102 (2%)

Gyms/Facilities:
Firestone Fieldhouse
Stotsenberg Track
Ralphs-Straus Tennis Center
Raleigh Runnels
Memorial Pool

Men's Varsity Sports:

Baseball
Basketball
Cross-Country
Golf
Tennis
Volleyball
Water Polo

Women's Varsity Sports:

Basketball
Cross-Country
Golf
Soccer
Swimming & Diving
Tennis
Volleyball

Club Sports:

Basketball
Flag Football
Soccer
Tennis
Volleyball

Intramurals:

Crew
Equestrian
Fencing
Field Hockey
Golf
Ice Hockey
Lacrosse
Rugby
Soccer (Men's)
Surfing
Ultimate Frisbee
Water Polo (Women's)

Athletic Fields

Eddy D. Field Stadium, Tari Frahm Rokus Field

Most Popular Sports

Basketball

Overlooked Teams

Baseball, cross-country, golf, swimming, and water polo

Best Place to Take a Walk

The safest bet to avoid breaking a sweat climbing stairs or hills is to walk in neat, flat ovals around the Stotsenberg Track. As a bonus, you are likely to walk into a celebrity or two, since a few are known to use Pepperdine's track.

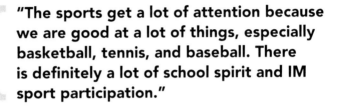

Students Speak Out On...
Athletics

"The sports get a lot of attention because we are good at a lot of things, especially basketball, tennis, and baseball. There is definitely a lot of school spirit and IM sport participation."

Q "Despite the athletic program's best efforts, men's **basketball is probably still the only sport that even draws a good-sized crowd**. Other sports that are fun and get overlooked are women's soccer, lacrosse, and men's and women's volleyball. Intramural basketball is popular, and it's a good time."

Q "**Unfortunately, Pepperdine doesn't have much school spirit when it comes to sports**. IMs are fairly big. I don't know about fan support, but lots of students are involved in IMs. Everyone goes to the basketball games. Those are fun, especially the big games."

Q "Our most talented teams, volleyball and water polo, are largely ignored because they don't get a lot of publicity. **If you want to get into intramural sports, there seems to be a lot of opportunity**, especially for basketball—but they don't seem to be incredibly popular."

Q "**Sports are huge, but more like admired from afar**, like a local team would be for a small town. We all go to the games, but no one really knows the players. They're a tight-knit group. Intramurals are where it's at, especially the rugby team. Very fun, very ferocious."

Q "The most popular sport at Pepperdine is the men's basketball team, which is interesting since they're really not that great. But, since **we have no football team**, this has become the social sports scene, or the games where you go to see people more than you do to see the game."

Q "**Varsity water polo, volleyball, and of course our basketball teams are always highly ranked**. IM sports are big too, but we lack any form of football, which kind of makes our sports department look ghetto. It is very easy just to go out and play an IM sport, if you are interested."

Q "**The sports system is small, though it is really good**. There are some IM sports, too, and there is always an opportunity to play. The sports teams are like Greek houses. They have initiation and whatnot. They are their own families."

Q "Sports are really big because **we have a lot of teams that are nationally ranked**, like our water polo team and our volleyball team. The biggest support, however, goes to the basketball team because their games are really the only social thing happening on campus."

Q "Pepperdine varsity sports win about seventy percent of their games. Despite our school's size, **we have seven national championships in NCAA sports**, which is amazing. Basketball is the big thing. IM sports are big, too."

Q "There is no football, so the main sport to follow is basketball. Many students don't support the athletics, though. **Most games are not crowded**."

The College Prowler Take On...
Athletics

Is the athletics scene big at Pepperdine, or isn't it? Students can't seem to agree. They do agree, though, that men's basketball is by far the most popular sport, essentially occupying the vacuum left by the absence of a football team. Yet the stands do not necessarily fill up for every game, and if basketball is really the featured attraction at Pepperdine, one is left to wonder just how unpopular some of the other sports must be.

Answer: pretty unpopular. Most students can easily attend Pepperdine for four years without ever seeing a water polo game or a tennis match, and the stands at the baseball games usually remain relatively barren—especially if you don't count the parents and scouts. It doesn't matter that some of these teams are nationally ranked; with the possible exception of the men's basketball team, students simply don't exhibit a whole lot of interest in their school's athletics. On the other hand, intramural and club sports are pretty popular. Maybe Pepperdine students are just more inclined to participate in the sporting life than they are to kick back and watch. At any rate, regardless of how good some of Pepperdine's teams are, people do not exhibit an overwhelming amount of support or enthusiasm for them.

The College Prowler® Grade on

Athletics: C+

A high grade in Athletics indicates that students have school spirit, that sports programs are respected, that games are well-attended, and that intramurals are a prominent part of student life.

Nightlife

The Lowdown On...
Nightlife

Club and Bar Prowler:
Popular Nightlife Spots!

Club Crawler:

Malibu may have a few bars, but to find clubs you've got to travel a little bit, usually to Santa Monica or the Sunset Strip. The happening places are pretty pricey, but a significant percentage of the Pepperdine student body wouldn't have it any other way.

Century Club

10131 Constellation Blvd., Century City

(310) 553-6000

Century Club has three floors with dancing on every one of them, and it is usually packed. If it's especially busy, you'll have to wait in line, which is annoying, as is the $20 cover. This is definitely a place for people who really want to dance; those looking to just stand around and shoot the breeze or have a few beers could probably find a better scene somewhere else.

➜

Joya

242 N Beverly Dr.,
Beverly Hills

(626) 372-4178

As the address suggests,
this place is a little ritzy.
Nonetheless, many
Pepperdine students are
willing to spend a little
dough to have a good time,
or to be seen having what
appears to be a good time
at a place where a bottle of
beer will set you back $12.
Once you've gotten on the
list and paid your cover
charge, you're free to sit
down in the bar and take in
the swanky décor, or you can
bolt directly upstairs to dance
the night away. They play
a good mix of all the music
you might expect to hear in a
place like this.

Whisky a Go-Go

8901 W Sunset Blvd., LA

(310) 652-4202

The Whisky is a legendary
dive on Sunset Strip, famous
for launching big-name
rock-n'-roll acts back in the
glorious '60s. It still hosts
a jam-packed schedule of
up-and-coming rock bands;
and it is generally crowded,
sweaty, casual, and loud.
Well, drinks are pretty cheap,
so what's not to like?

Bar Prowler:

Duke's Barefoot Bar

21150 Pacific Coast
Hwy., Malibu

(310) 317-0777

The Barefoot Bar at Duke's is
a bit of a drive down Pacific
Coast Highway, but it's worth
it. During happy hour they
have several half-price food
options in addition to the
cheap beers and Mai Tais.
All the while, you can take
in the sight of the waves
crashing up against the rocks
right outside the window;
for an even better view of
this activity, snag one of
the outdoor tables. Valet
parking can be annoying for
collegiate penny-pinchers,
but if you tell the guy you're
not there to eat dinner, but
rather to kill a little time in
the bar, he'll usually let you
bypass the whole valet thing.

Dume Room

29169 Heathercliff Rd.,
Suite 106, Malibu

(310) 457-9948

Named for nearby Point
Dume, the Dume Room is
a smoky little joint tucked
away among some innocuous
shops and businesses just up
the road from Pepperdine.
There are a couple of pool
tables in the back, and up
front there's the bar, where
during the day you'll find
the regulars, and at night
you're more likely to see
Pepperdine kids cramming
their way in to get a beer.

La Paz

4505 Las Virgenes Rd., Calabasas

(818) 880-8076

La Paz is a great little Mexican restaurant in Calabasas, 15 minutes from campus and very near where a lot of commuter students live. It also has a fun bar, and Friday afternoons you can count on seeing at least a few Pepperdine kids easing their way into the weekend there. On Sunday mornings you can partake of all the buffet-style Mexican food, margaritas, and champagne you want for $20. Olé!

Malibu Inn

22969 Pacific Coast Hwy., Malibu

(310) 456-6060

The Inn is the old standby for Pepperdine students. It offers live music and a great location right next to campus. On Tuesday nights and weekends, the place is generally packed. Expect a cover charge, and, like anywhere else in the area, fairly pricey drinks. All in all, it's a laid-back environment and the place to go if there's nothing else to do.

Maloney's

1000 Gayley Ave., Westwood Village

(310) 208-1942

This bar brings in young professionals, Pepperdine students, and of course, UCLA students. This is your typical college hangout, with an oak bar and cozy enclaves. Lines can get a little crazy after 11 p.m. Thursday–Saturday, so try to arrive early if you can.

Roxy Theatre

9009 W Sunset Blvd., West Hollywood

(310) 278-9457

www.theroxyonsunset.com

This is a great place to catch a show from rock music to pop. There is a two drink mininum, and tickets can be purchased at the box office or through *www.ticketmaster.com*. Roxy offers really good food (not cheap), a cool ambiance with a glowing bar, and a cool crowd.

Saddle Ranch

8371 W. Sunset Blvd., West Hollywood

(323) 656-2007

This is a country-western chophouse with open-fire pits, fake horses, and hay bales. Feels like Texas in here! This is also a place where you can chill and watch the many TVs, and hangout on the outdoor patio where you can roast marshmallows by the fire pit.

Sunset Room

1430 N Cahuenga Blvd., Hollywood

(323) 463-0004

Sunset Room is exactly what you think about when you think Hollywood. Celebrities have parties here. This place is extremely posh, with good-looking people, great music, and an especially nice ambiance. Don't forget to bring your wallet, though. DInner reservations are recommended, also.

Bars Close At:

2:00 a.m.

Primary Areas with Nightlife:

Santa Monica and Sunset Boulevards

Cheapest Place to Get a Drink:

La Paz at happy hour

Other Places to Check Out:

Geoffrey's Malibu

House of Blues

Rainbow Room

Sky Bar

The Standard

The Viper Room

Favorite Drinking Games:

Beer Pong

Card Games (A$$hole, Kings)

Century Club

Power Hour

Quarters

Sake Bombing

Students Speak Out On...
Nightlife

"There are no parties on campus. Pepperdine is a dry campus. When a Pepperdine student has a party off campus, chances are that it will be broken up before midnight."

Q "No parties on campus, unless you count your little ole' dorm room (and I don't). The Malibu Inn is basically the spot in Malibu, with the LA nightlife looming down the freeway. Sports teams and fraternities usually host a round of parties during the year—but count on bringing your own booze or paying your way in. **It's not cheap to drink here**."

Q "Being a dry campus in a small town means that most parties are held in the apartments or houses of people who live off campus. **From what I've heard, the club scene isn't all that fabulous, and the bars are pretty seedy**. If you're a hard-core partier, this is probably not the school for you."

Q "There are no parties on campus, except in your ten-by-ten-foot dorm room. **There are only two worthwhile bars off campus, the Dume Room and the Malibu Inn**. The Inn can be fun, but you will get sick of it. To find any good nightlife, you will have to make the 30- to 45-minute drive into downtown LA."

Q "Too many Pepperdine students show up at one party. Bars and clubs are fun, but **they're expensive (cover charges are ridiculous)**. Sunset has a whole bunch of clubs and bars—though the tendency for people to 'dress up' was never my scene. I preferred the Dume Room myself, though it's a somewhat sketchy dive bar. The Whisky a Go-Go is cool, as well as the Roxy Theatre."

Q "If by 'parties,' you mean alcohol consumed furtively while hiding in your dorm or suite, then yes, **parties on campus are big**."

Q "There's really only one bar in Malibu, and that's the Malibu Inn. It's pretty good, and a lot of the upperclassmen hang out there in the evenings or for parties. **Most Pep parties take place at people's houses in the Valley**. Hollywood has tons of clubs for dancing and partying, as does Santa Monica."

Q "When I first started at Pepperdine, I went out two or three nights during the week, as well as Friday and Saturday. **My grades suffered, though**. Whoops!"

Q "Try Maloney's over by UCLA. **Two-for-one drinks on Sunday nights**—just hope you don't have an early Monday morning class! Sunset Strip is loaded with clubs and bars. You can find just about anything in LA."

Q "The **Malibu Inn and La Paz are where everyone goes on Tuesday and Friday nights**, respectively. The Inn is a classic small pub with live music. La Paz is this Mexican restaurant through the canyon that has happy hour from 4 to 7 p.m."

Q "We have the Malibu Inn, where lots of people hang out. Sometimes, **big musicians will just randomly play** a set without any notice. We're 40 minutes from the world-famous Sunset Strip! No one can beat that!"

Q "Well, in Malibu there is the Inn . . . oh, and the Inn . . . oh yeah, you might want to check out a place called the Inn, as far as bars and clubs are concerned. There is plenty to do in the city; **you just have to drive about 20 or 30 minutes to Sunset**. There are always house parties, too, at various houses."

The College Prowler Take On...
Nightlife

Students' opinions differ according to what they expect of the term "nightlife." If good nightlife means posh, exclusive nightclubs and bars with horrendous cover charges but a happenin' scene indoors, then the nightlife for any student living near LA is going to be pretty good. For Pepperdiners, most of these places will require at least a half-hour commute, however, as well as a fairly handsome budget. If a good nightlife means fun local parties and on-campus merriment, forget it. On the other hand, if you'd rather spend your weekends doing and seeing interesting, non-alcoholic things, you've got all of Santa Monica, Hollywood, and LA to explore. The Student Government Association and University Ministries also sponsor plenty of wholesome entertainment on campus that, while not really popular with most students, do attract a loyal following.

But if you have your heart set on partying up a storm for the next four years, it may be a tad disconcerting that first Friday night when you step outside your freshman dorm, ready for the party to start, only to be greeted by the faint chirping of crickets and the thumping of Bibles. If this concerns you, you should either get yourself an ID for the swanky bars and clubs, or else limit your weekend excitement to the intermittent, overcrowded, and quickly-broken-up misadventures that Pepperdine considers house parties.

The College Prowler® Grade on

Nightlife: B-

A high grade in Nightlife indicates that there are many bars and clubs in the area that are easily accessible and affordable. Other determining factors include the number of options for the under-21 crowd and the prevalence of house parties.

Greek Life

The Lowdown On...
Greek Life

Number of Fraternities:	**Undergrad Men in Fraternities:**
4	24%
Number of Sororities:	**Undergrad Women in Sororities:**
7	29%

➜

Fraternities:

Beta Theta Pi

Psi Upsilon

Sigma Chi

Sigma Phi Epsilon

Sororities:

Alpha Phi

Delta Delta Delta

Delta Gamma

Gamma Phi Beta

Kappa Alpha Theta

Kappa Kappa Gamma

Pi Beta Phi

Other Greek Organizations:

Greek Council

Greek Peer Advisors

Interfraternity Council

Order of Omega

Panhellenic Council

Did You Know?

The number of fraternities fell from five to four recently, when **the administration banned Sigma Nu's local chapter from Pepperdine forever**. The controversial frat—commonly recognized to be the wildest Greek group on campus, though at Pepperdine that isn't saying much—had been placed on probation a number of times, but they finally threw one rule-breaking party too many.

It has become a tradition at Pepperdine for the various Greek chapters to **decorate a big rock placed rather incongruously in the middle of campus**, usually to promote their rush events. Each chapter takes turns adopting the rock for 24 hours; during the night they decorate the rock (in ways that grow increasingly elaborate with each passing year), and members of the chapter take shifts "guarding" it over the course of the following day.

Students Speak Out On...
Greek Life

"Greek life can dominate the social scene during big events throughout the year, like Homecoming. But for the most part, you can separate yourself from Greek life very easily. There are no Greek houses on campus, which makes it less in your face."

Q "**The Greek life component of Pepperdine is definitely a very visible part of campus life**. Most of the posters you see around campus are for Greek events, and my freshman year, I often felt that I hardly met anyone not in a sorority or fraternity. However, because Pepperdine has no houses, the Greeks are not removed from the campus in any way, and you don't feel as if they were incredibly cliquey or exclusive about their friends."

Q "I actually know of **many girls and guys who disaffiliated**."

Q "I would not say Greek life dominates the social scene, since **all Pepperdine parties are basically a secret** anyway. In terms of on-campus activities, though, the Greeks do hold the lion's share."

Q "The **Greek life is stupid**."

Q "I don't see how it could not dominate the social scene. **Most of the events on campus revolve around Greeks**, but you can find your own groups without pledging. Of course, you'll have a much better time if you do!"

Q "I just recently escaped the evil clutches of my sorority, so a note to the ladies: it is hard to make a big decision like joining a sorority during the first few weeks of college. Before you make that big decision, know yourself well, and don't fall for all of their well-conceived lines. **It's a lifelong commitment if you join**, and they don't stress the implications of that enough."

Q "**I was in a sorority, and my advice to a girl thinking about doing the same is: don't**. It became a waste of time and money by the end, and I found as the years went forward that the reputation of my sorority shifted right out from underneath me. By the year I graduated, I had few friends left in the sorority, as my interests diverged from those of the group. You can still be a part of the social scene without having to join a sorority or fraternity."

Q "I am not in a sorority. I always wanted to join, but I transferred in during spring, and since there is no spring rush, I wasn't even able to consider joining one until the fall. By then, however, I made a ton of friends—some involved with Greek life and some not—and I realized that **it was possible to have a great social life without being Greek**. I have never regretted not joining. My roommate was president of her sorority, so I got to deal with the positives and negatives of sorority life, and I wasn't even in one!"

Q "**Have you ever seen _Legally Blonde_**? That's my sorority, to a T."

Q "Because it is such a small school, Greek life does dominate the entire social scene. I rushed my freshman year, but if I had to do it over again, I would have waited until at least my second year. I love my sorority, but **you do get stereotyped according to which sorority you pledge**."

Q "I am not in the Greek system, and **I'm not a real big fan of paying for friends**, but a lot of people are, and they like it."

Q "Greek life is sort of a big part of the campus. It is not the typical Deep South Greek system. We do not have houses, but there are people who live with their 'sisters' in apartments or houses. **I'm in a sorority, and it's the best thing I could have done**. It is a great way to meet people and really get involved. It's also a great way to find out about the social events and parties on the weekends. All of the sororities get along really well, and the frats are really cool, too. It's definitely not a typical Greek system, though."

Q "Greek life completely dominates social life. **It's only competition is spiritual life**, which is huge, but it is often very cliquish. Pepperdine seems like a fashion show."

Q "I'm in a fraternity, Sigma Phi Epsilon—a great move on my part, but not necessary. **My best friends at Pepperdine aren't in my fraternity**, they're guys I met in my dorm."

Q "The people in the Greek system always have something to do, which is a major bonus. But the whole Greek thing just wasn't for me. **Because the campus is so small, I didn't feel like I had to join a frat to make friends**."

The College Prowler Take On...
Greek Life

Some college kids join fraternities or sororities and forge lifelong friendships. Others condemn Greek life with notable fervor. Still others remain out of the fray, altogether disinterested. Such is the case with just about any university, but at Pepperdine the Greek debate seems exaggerated. When many Pepperdine kids already characterize the student body, in general, as arrogant and snobbish, you can just guess how they feel about the fraternity and sorority members on campus. Also, when those same students complain that Pepperdine is too small, and too like a country club, it makes one wonder: what's the point of joining a Greek group? Wouldn't it be something like joining a fraternity within a fraternity?

One answer to that question is that, yes, many students do want to belong to an exclusive group that distinguishes itself among an already exclusive student body. Cynics are wont to define this behavior as "buying friends." But the other thing to remember is that Pepperdine's Greek system is a lot different than other schools'. Several of the frats and sororities place a far greater emphasis on such unglamorous aims as school spirit, community service, and Christian worship than they do on social mixers, beer bongs, and formals. Also, many would say that Pepperdine's Greek system is practically the only vehicle through which to remain plugged into campus life for your full four years—especially if you move off campus at some point, as most students do.

The College Prowler® Grade on
Greek Life: B+

A high grade in Greek Life indicates that sororities and fraternities are not only present, but also active on campus. Other determining factors include the variety of houses available and the respect the Greek community receives from the rest of the campus.

Drug Scene

The Lowdown On...
Drug Scene

Most Prevalent Drugs on Campus:
Marijuana's about as wild as most students dare to get on campus. Other drug use—cocaine and ecstasy are the main ones you hear about—takes place either off campus or very furtively.

Liquor-Related Referrals:
100

Liquor-Related Arrests:
6

Drug-Related Referrals:
15

Drug-Related Arrests:
3

Drug Counseling Programs

The Student Counseling Center

(310) 506-4210

Services: Individual counseling, support groups, psychological consultation and care

The Health Center

(310) 506-4316

Services: Literature on alcohol and drug abuse, counseling, and referrals

The Wellness Program

(310) 506-7592

Services: Health education and promotion, spiritual guidance, and counseling

Students Speak Out On...
Drug Scene

> **"Drugs are not hard to find, but they're very easy to stay away from."**

Q "I know it is there, but to what degree I am not really sure because **I have not really been confronted with it**."

Q "**There are a lot of underground pot smokers**. Some cocaine, apparently, though I never saw it myself."

Q "There is definitely a good percentage of students on campus that smoke weed, and I'm sure there is other drug use. **But, it's nothing out of control**. Alcohol use, like on any campus, is definitely present. Not to say everyone drinks, but I bet over half the student population does."

Q "**I'm blind to all of that type of stuff**."

Q "I really don't know anything about that. After a while, you get the idea of whom to go to for these kinds of things, but **not a lot of it can happen on campus without the person getting caught**."

Q "I don't know much about it. **Campus is pretty clean when it comes to drugs**."

Q "**It definitely exists** in full effect!"

Q "There's not much of a drug scene, really. **At least, I never noticed one**."

Q   "**I think I got stoned once**, maybe twice."

Q   "There are drugs. If you're into it, you can find the scene. However, **this is a conservative Christian campus, so the drug scene tends to be hidden**."

Q   "**It's a Christian school**. Not many do drugs."

Q   "Ecstasy used to be a very big drug on campus, but now cocaine is more of a problem. **A lot of students at Pepperdine are rich, so high-priced drugs are very much a problem**."

Q   "It's here **if you want it**."

The College Prowler Take On...
Drug Scene

Reading the disparity of student perceptions of the Pepperdine drug scene tells a lot about drug use on campus. Some have never noticed much of a drug scene at all, while others insist that expensive drugs are "very big" on campus. A logical inference is that whatever serious drugs students snort, swallow, or inhale are being used either off campus, or in an extremely covert manner. If they weren't, it would not be long before a sharp RA or Public Safety officer would catch the offending students.

Despite the conservative Christian atmosphere and campus regulations, Pepperdine is still college, and many students will still experiment with drugs. But compared to other college campuses, drug use at Pepperdine is minimal. Even the long-haired guy in the beat-up van with Vermont plates and a "Free Tibet" bumper sticker is liable to pass on grass. You just never can tell. And despite the talk about some students using cocaine and other serious drugs, it's virtually impossible to find yourself in such an environment—unless you intentionally put yourself there.

The College Prowler® Grade on

Drug Scene: B+

A high grade in the Drug Scene indicates that drugs are not a noticeable part of campus life; drug use is not visible, and no pressure to use them seems to exist.

Campus Strictness

The Lowdown On...
Campus Strictness

What Are You Most Likely to Get Caught Doing on Campus?

- Drinking
- Having a member of the opposite sex in your room or suite after 1 a.m.

Students Speak Out On...
Campus Strictness

> **"Can't drink on campus. Can't get drunk off campus. End of story."**

Q "Campus police are pretty strict. **Not only is it a dry campus, it is religious! Double whammy**! Don't worry, I still found a way to sneak drinks in the dorms on the weekends. Where there's a will, there's a way!"

Q "The campus police are incredibly strict about drugs and drinking, and **if they find alcohol in your room, you'll have to go before the board to defend yourself**. One or two students have even been expelled since I've been at Pepperdine for selling or possessing drugs. That being said, the RAs aren't always as strict as the campus police on these sorts of issues. You could have an RA who couldn't care less about your drinking in the room, or one who will report you to the Judicial Board on your first infraction. It's just the luck of the draw."

Q "A lot **depends on who you get for an RA**."

Q "Very strict. Don't even think about drinking and driving on campus. **It totally depends on how much your RA will take when it comes to parties**. If she's a pushover, you can basically do whatever you want to. The other side of the RA situation is getting kicked off of campus."

Q "They are strict, but they are not looking to get you in trouble. **If you do something stupid, it is your own fault**."

Q "From what I hear, **Public Safety is not very strict about drugs and drinking**."

"I would classify Pepperdine as very strict, **but you only get caught if you are stupid or very unlucky**."

"**Extremely strict, though it does depend on how much money your parents have**. There seems to be a no-tolerance policy. When you're caught, you're kicked out. I've heard stories of lesser punishments, though, when money has been involved."

"Police are very strict about drugs and drinking on campus. It's up to your RA, though, if he or she will turn you in. **Most of the time, they'll give you a warning before turning you over** to the discipline board."

"Pepperdine is a dry campus. **No drugs, alcohol, or anything allowed**. It is very dry, and they are fairly strict."

"There are ways around the rules. It has been done, but I have also gotten in trouble. **You just have to be careful**."

"**Getting caught drinking is pretty serious**, but of course, we do it."

"**They are really, really, really strict**. You can't drink on campus, or even get caught being intoxicated on campus."

"You will get kicked out of school if you get a DUI, even if you got it off campus. The local police report it back to the campus police! It is a dry campus, but people drink on campus all the time. **You just have to be careful. We definitely know how to have a good time here**."

"Campus police are very strict. This is no state school. They don't look the other way. **If you're busted, say bye-bye to Pepperdine**."

The College Prowler Take On...
Campus Strictness

Students almost unanimously identify Pepperdine as inflexible when it comes to enforcing campus rules and regulations. Even things you do off campus can get you in trouble, so you really have to take pains to watch your step wherever you go. Further complicating matters are a few particularly stringent policies, such as the one that prohibits guests of the opposite sex in any dorm room past midnight, or in any suite between one and ten in the morning. A uniquely lenient RA may not write you up for such an infraction, but he or she will certainly send the guest packing—even if it's Mom or Dad stopping by to bring you your favorite pillow at nine in the morning. Also, "quiet hours" extend from 10 p.m. to 10 a.m., which means that if you raise a ruckus, or even a semi-ruckus, during this period, you are likely to get a visit from Public Safety or your RA. Given these restrictions, it's not hard to understand why on-campus partying does not exactly flourish at Pepperdine.

Nevertheless, students also insist that, if you can manage to hide whatever you're doing from Public Safety and from the watchful eyes of your RA, you can get away with a lot. Just know that if you do get caught, for example, drinking in your dorm room, there will be a price to pay. One infraction will put you on academic probation and endanger any scholarships or aid you receive from the University. One or two infractions after that, and you could find yourself in a heap of trouble.

The College Prowler® Grade on

Campus
Strictness: D

A high Campus Strictness grade implies an overall lenient atmosphere; police and RAs are fairly tolerant, and the administration's rules are flexible.

Parking

The Lowdown On...
Parking

Approximate Parking Permit Cost:
Free

Student Parking Lot?
Yes

Freshmen Allowed to Park?
Yes

Pepperdine University Parking Services:
Contact Public Safety at (310) 506-4700, or visit *www.pepperdine.edu/ publicsafety/parking.*

Parking Permits

Any undergraduate student can get a free parking permit.

Common Parking Tickets

No Parking Zone: $20

Handicapped Zone: $280

Fire Lane: $20

Did You Know?

Best Places to Find a Parking Spot
Firestone Fieldhouse parking lot

Good Luck Getting a Parking Spot Here!
Anywhere else

The Boot: A student who has gotten five tickets in a year, or one who has committed any serious parking offense, may find upon returning to his or her car that Public Safety has equipped it with a bright orange wheel-locking device called a "boot." That thing doesn't come off until you pay an "immobilization fee" on top of all outstanding penalties.

Students Speak Out On...
Parking

"Parking is free, which is nice. However, there is a nice 15-minute walk to the closest parking lot. Oh, did I mention that Pepperdine is one big hill?"

Q "**Learn parallel parking**. Now."

Q "The parking scene is one of the worst parts about Pepperdine because **it's very overcrowded**, especially in the main residential lot and the streets around main campus."

Q "**Parking can be easy, and it can be horrible**."

Q "The only two places where you can always find parking are down by the Fieldhouse (about 200 stairs down from main campus), or in the Drescher Graduate Campus parking garage. Public Safety is pretty strict about parking—**students are always getting ticketed for parking in the wrong place**."

Q "**There are not enough spaces**, what with everyone bringing their cars to school."

Q "**Parking is a piece of cake**. It's not overcrowded, at least from what I see on weekends. Students park near their dorms or in parking lots surrounding the campus. If you can, I suggest bringing a car, because you may want to drive to Santa Monica."

Q "**Get to school a half hour before class** if you want a spot."

Q "Parking is horrible. If you park before 6 a.m., you can get a nice spot. But any time after eight, you're parking down at the Firestone Fieldhouse parking lot. **Be prepared to climb hundreds of stairs**."

Q "Parking has become a nightmare for me recently—**too many students, not enough spaces**."

Q "Parking can be kind of a pain in the butt, but there is parking. If you live on campus, it is easier to park than if you live off. Just make sure you park in the right spot— they can ticket you. **Cars are always safe, though. Over half the people drive Mercedes and BMWs, so it must be fairly safe**."

Q "**Parking can be a pain, but you always find a place**. You might have to walk a bit, but it is nothing you can't handle."

Q "**I hope you can parallel park on a hill**."

Q "Depending on where you live, it can be quite a hike to get to the lots. But you can usually find a spot to park, even if it does mean **circling around for a little bit and praying to the parking gods for a close spot**."

The College Prowler Take On...
Parking

Parking is undoubtedly the source of many a Pepperdine student's complaints. If you get to campus early or late enough in the day, you can find a good spot, but getting your car in it might entail—brace yourself—parallel parking. Not only that, but you often will have to parallel park on an incline or a decline, which helps explain why fender benders seem remarkably common. At other times, the only reliable place to park is down at the Firestone Fieldhouse parking lot, which doesn't require parallel parking, but does mean you will probably have to hike to class.

Students whine an awful lot about parking, but in truth it isn't that bad. Pepperdine spoils its students in so many ways that the inconvenience of parking seems like a disaster, but, for one thing, the parking permit's free. For another, you can always find a parking space; you just might have a torturous 10-minute hike up the hill ahead of you to get to class, which probably means that you will arrive sweaty, irritable, and grumbling about the parking on campus. But, if you allow yourself just a little extra time on your drive to school—which is, I must admit, a curiously difficult thing to do in college—you can park your car in the rarely-full parking lot at the Firestone Fieldhouse and then wait for a shuttle to come by and whisk you off to class.

The College Prowler® Grade on

Parking: B-

A high grade in this section indicates that parking is both available and affordable, and that parking enforcement isn't overly severe.

Transportation

The Lowdown On...
Transportation

Ways to Get Around Town:
On Campus
Waves Shuttle Service
8:00 a.m.–10:30 p.m.
(310) 506-4802

Student Service Officer
Escort Program
8:00 p.m.–2:30 a.m.
or anytime by request through
Public Safety
(310) 506-4442

Public Transportation
CalTrans
(213) 897-4867

Taxi Cabs
Malibu Cab
(310) 456-0500

Malibu A Taxi
(310) 317-0048

United Checker Cab Company
(310) 834-1121

Yellow Cab
(310) 808-1000 or
(800) 200-1085

Bell Cab
(888) 235-5222 or
(800) 666-6664

Beverly Hills Cab Company
(310) 273-6611 or
(800) 273-6611

(Taxi Cabs, continued)

Independent Taxi,
(323) 666-0050 or
(800) 521-8294

Car Rentals

Alamo
local: (310) 649-2242
national: (800) 327-9633
www.alamo.com

Avis
local: (310) 646-5600
national: (800) 831-2847
www.avis.com

Budget
local: (310) 670-1744
national: (800) 527-0700
www.budget.com

Dollar
local: (213) 487-0303
national: (800) 800-4000
www.dollar.com

Enterprise
local: (310) 836-3336
national: (800) 736-8222
www.enterprise.com

Hertz
local: (310) 645-7001
national: (800) 654-3131
www.hertz.com

National
local: (310) 417-8240
national: (800) 227-7368
www.nationalcar.com

Best Ways to Get Around Town

Borrow your buddy's car

Bum a ride

Drive! It's LA! (Well, the LA area)

Use the off-campus shuttle provided by SGA, (310) 506-4360.

Ways to Get Out of Town:

Airlines Serving Los Angeles

Alaska Airlines
(800) 252-7522
www.alaskaair.com

American Airlines
(800) 433-7300
www.aa.com

Continental
(800) 523-3273
www.continental.com

Delta
(800) 221-1212
www.delta.com

Northwest
(800) 225-2525
www.nwa.com

Southwest
(800) 435-9792
www.southwest.com

TWA
(800) 221-2000
www.twa.com

United
(800) 241-6522
www.united.com

US Airways
(800) 428-4322
www.usairways.com

Airport

Los Angeles
International Airport
(310) 642-7008

LAX is about 40 miles away,
and, depending on traffic, it
can take anywhere from 50
to 90 minutes to get there.

How to Get to the Airport

Airport Shuttle
(310) 317-1992
$45, plus $7 for each
additional passenger.

Road Runner Shuttle
(805) 389-8196, $35

Primetime Shuttles
(800) 733-8267.
With the Pepperdine
discount, Primetime (Red
Vans) costs $27, plus $11 for
each additional passenger.

A cab ride to the airport costs
$35 for up to four people
with Malibu Cab.

Greyhound

The closest Greyhound bus
terminal is through Malibu
Canyon in Thousand Oaks,
about 13 miles from campus.
Call (805) 449-7265 for
schedule information.

www.greyhound.com

Greyhound Trailways
Bus Terminal
707 E. Thousand Oaks
Blvd. 11
Thousand Oaks, CA

Amtrak

The nearest Amtrak station
is in LA, about 25 miles
away. Call (213) 624-0171
for information.

www.amtrak.com

LA Amtrak Train Station
1605 W. Olympic Blvd.
Los Angeles, CA

Travel Agents

Waterways Travel
22611 Pacific Coast
Hwy., Malibu
(310) 456-7744

Westways World Travel
21225 Pacific Coast
Hwy. #C, Malibu
(310) 451-5323

Malibu Lake Travel
29251 Circle Dr.,
Agoura Hills
(818) 991-3324

Students Speak Out On...
Transportation

"I think there's a bus system. It's pretty tough to have a satisfying life in Malibu without a car, though Pepperdine does run a shuttle down to the grocery store. So I guess if you made enough friends with cars, it wouldn't be so bad."

Q "**The shuttle system is definitely unreliable**. One time, my friend had to wait three hours to get picked up from an innocent Malibu Yo' run."

Q "There is no public transportation. **Bring your car, or suffer social suicide**."

Q "**Public transportation is your friends** and roommates."

Q "I believe some people make it work, but if you are sans vehicle, **the majority of people I know get around by riding with friends**."

Q "**The buses come directly on campus, and you can get anywhere** on them, but it might take a while. You can almost always bum rides from friends."

Q "**Public transportation only comes into town** to ship in and out blue-collar workers to do the jobs white collars won't."

Q "**I never used public transportation**."

Q "Public transportation is **almost nonexistent**."

Q "Public transportation is not very good. **Get a car**."

Q "**There is no real public transit** or transportation to speak of. You must either have a car, borrow one, or find someone willing to drive you."

Q "They have **shuttles that go around school**, and one that takes you to Ralphs across the street. I suggest bringing a car."

Q "There are taxis in town, and LA has a subway system. **Most kids have a car**. I definitely recommend bringing a car."

The College Prowler Take On...
Transportation

Public transportation at Pepperdine is about as popular as that high-pitched squirrelly guy on *Saved by the Bell*. The resounding opinion of Pep students is that the school's off-campus shuttles are inconvenient and unreliable, and most students are oblivious to LA's subway and bus options. Their resounding advice, therefore, is to bring a car, and if that's just not possible, plan to make friends with vehicle-equipped students as quickly as possible.

One cool alternative to a car, if you only need something to scoot around campus and into Malibu, is to get one of those motorized scooters. A few students and even some professors have them—and just imagine how quickly you can climb the social ladder by giving free rides to class! As far as getting yourself to and from the airport, a lot of students rely on the Primetime Shuttles, or "Red Vans." Yet the Malibu Cab company charges only a few bucks more, and that's for a group of four travelers. Just don't count exclusively—or much at all, for that matter—on public transportation to get you out and about during your tenure at Pepperdine.

The College Prowler® Grade on

Transportation: D

A high grade for Transportation indicates that campus buses, public buses, cabs, and rental cars are readily-available and affordable. Other determining factors include proximity to an airport and the necessity of transportation.

Weather

The Lowdown On...
Weather

Average Temperature:

Fall:	65°F
Winter:	56°F
Spring:	60°F
Summer:	70°F

Average Precipitation:

Fall:	2.3 in.
Winter:	1.2 in.
Spring:	5.1 in.
Summer:	0.2 in.

Students Speak Out On...
Weather

> **"The weather is like paradise. Of course it still rains and gets cold, but it is usually beautiful, especially on the beaches of Malibu."**

💬 "**The weather is perfect**. It's Malibu."

💬 "It's Malibu! **There's a reason that some of the richest people in the country live here**."

💬 "The typical day in Malibu is clear, sunny, and about 75 degrees. **It's just gorgeous, but mild enough that you can pretty much wear what you want**. In the winter, it can get fairly windy and rainy, but never that bad. In terms of clothing, though, just keep in mind the profile of a Pepperdine student is very wealthy, and most of them dress the part. If you don't fit into this rich, fashionable category, you may feel more than a little frumpy as you walk around campus in jeans and a T-shirt."

💬 "**The weather is predominantly sunny, and often a bit breezy**. I wasn't too keen on the weather, as I appreciate the rain myself. But as far as clothes go, bring layers and different options for shoes (sandals, sneakers, and so on). The winters have their fair share of rainstorms and mudslides. Bring a jacket."

💬 "Someone once told me you will want layers, because often it can be warm and SoCal-sunny during the day, but then get very chilly at night. **You will want beach clothes as well as sweaters and stuff**."

Q "Very hot through the summer and into September, but besides that it's very temperate. **Think jeans, T-shirts, and flip-flops: all designer and expensive, of course.**"

Q "**Sixty percent of the time, it is 80 degrees with the sun shining**. The other 40 percent is nighttime."

Q "It is not 70 degrees and sunny everyday. **It does rain in Southern California, and it can get cold.**"

Q "**It's 70 to 80 degrees all year round**, and it barely rains."

Q "**It's Southern California—great weather**. We do get a marine layer along the ocean."

Q "**It is the usual California weather: no real winter, but maybe a little rain**. It can get a little chilly, but never really bad. It doesn't get really hot in the summer either, because you are close to the ocean. You are just across Pacific Coast Highway from the ocean."

Q "It's cold to me always—I was born and raised in Southern Cali, where it's always warm. **But since Malibu is on the beach, the air is always stabilized to about 50 or 60 degrees**. I hate that. I'm always freezing. However, we have some warm days in the beginning of September and late April."

Q "If you were judging solely on weather, nowhere in America beats Malibu. I slept with the windows open every night that it didn't rain, and **it only rained four times in the eight months that I was there**."

Q "Well, sometimes it's foggy since the school is about one mile from the ocean, but it is generally breezy, pleasant, and sunny—**beach weather**!"

The College Prowler Take On...
Weather

The made-to-order Malibu weather nicely augments Pepperdine's thrilling vistas to create a uniquely beautiful environment. No wonder most students find little about the weather to gripe and grumble about. The average temperatures vary by only five to ten degrees with the changing seasons, making for a very clement climate. People from, say, New England might bellyache about the lack of seasonal diversity. It is true that Malibu seems to live in a perpetual springtime, but I think most would agree that spring is a pretty good season to be stuck in year-round.

That being said, for a couple of short stretches during the year, the weather can get a bit more interesting. Remember to bring some warm clothes to protect you from the morning fog during the winter months, and an umbrella for the rare but sudden rains that usually hit around January and can cause flashfloods and rockslides on the Pacific Coast Highway and Malibu Canyon. (These are infrequent but potentially hazardous intrusions on Pepperdine's otherwise sunny disposition.) On the flipside, in August the weather can turn so warm that dorm dwellers throw open their windows, set all their personal fans to high, and kick away the comforters at night. Again, such weather is an exception to the rule—that nearly every day finds the sun shining mildly, the palm trees swaying gently in the breeze, and the girls flitting around in short skirts.

The College Prowler® Grade on

Weather: A+

A high Weather grade designates that temperatures are mild and rarely reach extremes, that the campus tends to be sunny rather than rainy, and that weather is fairly consistent rather than unpredictable.

Report Card Summary

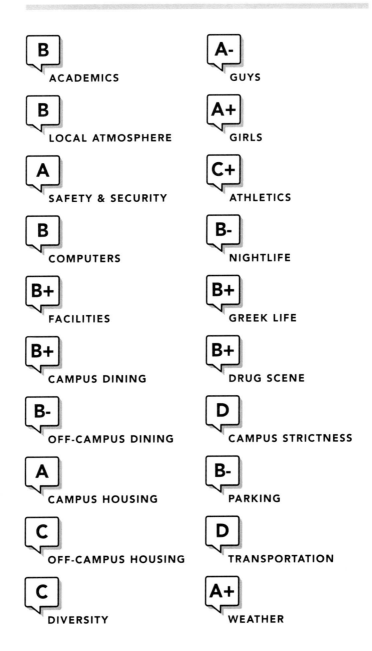

B ACADEMICS	**A-** GUYS
B LOCAL ATMOSPHERE	**A+** GIRLS
A SAFETY & SECURITY	**C+** ATHLETICS
B COMPUTERS	**B-** NIGHTLIFE
B+ FACILITIES	**B+** GREEK LIFE
B+ CAMPUS DINING	**B+** DRUG SCENE
B- OFF-CAMPUS DINING	**D** CAMPUS STRICTNESS
A CAMPUS HOUSING	**B-** PARKING
C OFF-CAMPUS HOUSING	**D** TRANSPORTATION
C DIVERSITY	**A+** WEATHER

Overall Experience

Students Speak Out On...
Overall Experience

{ **"The religious emphasis was a bit much for me, but the quality people that I met and the amazing experiences, both academic and social, were worth it for me. I'm glad to have gone to Pepperdine."**

Q "**Pepperdine is the best university in existence, and I'll tell that to anyone who asks**. The opportunities given to students here are just awesome, most significantly in the area of international programs. I've been lucky enough to participate in three of them, and they completely changed my life and made my college experience."

Q "My experiences at Pepperdine were bittersweet. **Go into this school knowing that it is an expensive private school and nothing else**."

Q "My overall experience at Pepperdine was very positive, though **no school is without its politics or its groups of students that you just won't understand**. Freshman year was exciting, as the administration worked hard to acclimate recently-graduated high school seniors to the social and academic workload of being in college. There are fun student-organized events, including a day at Disneyland and free movies. Sophomore year was amazing on several levels, but mostly because I was studying abroad in London. The study abroad program at Pepperdine is incredibly strong and well established. I know several students who went to Buenos Aires, Florence, and Heidelberg, and who were reluctant to come back home. Junior and senior years at Pepperdine were concentrated on working toward my major. My professors and peers challenged me daily."

Q "**I left Pepperdine after three semesters**, and I wish I hadn't."

Q "**Though I had very few problems with Pepperdine, one that comes to mind is the lack of courses offered** for the school's more obscure degrees (specifically creative writing). And though Pepperdine lists itself as a liberal arts school, being in the creative arts myself, I found that the University gave very little support to its creative writers. The humanities department has fallen prey to major cutbacks."

Q "It's an amazing place, **but it feels like a bubble most of the time**."

Q "My experience has been great. I love it, and I don't wish I were anywhere else. **If you're worried about being homesick, don't be**. I got over it in a hurry. I went a long way and knew nobody, and I had a blast. I can't recommend it strongly enough."

"Truthfully, I really love the people that I met at Pepperdine and the experiences that I had. I was a cheerleader, a camp counselor, in a sorority, and really made a lot of friends my first two years there. However, Pepperdine is a really small school, and **for some people, there is only so much growing that can be done at this institution**. That was the case for me. The experiences that I had and the friends that I made I will no doubt keep for the rest of my life, and for that I am grateful, but I felt the way many people have felt: that it was no longer the place for me. A lot of my friends have also transferred to bigger schools. I did a year of community college, and I will be transferring to USC in the fall."

"**For me, Pepperdine is like a vacation where you have to work**, but you can balance anything you want to do. The people are great, teachers actually care, and there are tons of things to do. I sometimes find myself wondering what I would be doing if I was somewhere else, not because I don't love the people here, but as far as my program is concerned. I wonder if I could be spending my time more efficiently. Either you love it, or you don't. I love the school and the people, but there are just some times when you wonder: what if?"

"Get yourself involved in different things, and you'll love it; don't, and you won't. **Pepperdine has the best international programs around**. The most important thing about Pepperdine, though, is that it's a private, Christian school. You are required to go to weekly convocation in order to graduate. It's a place and a time where you will be tested the most in your life."

"I'm having a great time at Pepperdine. **I only wish I was elsewhere when I miss big Southern football**. It's a once-in-a-lifetime experience, though. Also, I should note that Pep has amazing overseas programs that about half the students take advantage of. I'm going to London next spring to study."

Q "At first, I wished I had gone elsewhere. It was truly culture shock to be with so many wealthy white people. **I don't think most people are open-minded here. The kids are very sheltered and spoiled**. Don't get me wrong—they aren't all like that, but many are. I just felt cheated out of the college experience. I thought college was to find out others' points of view and to become better rounded, but at Pepperdine, people are very conservative. The only thing that makes me think I made a good choice has been my professors. They are great! I could not imagine getting a better education anywhere."

Q "**I still think Pepperdine has been the best college I could have gone to**; I have made amazing friends and have had wonderful, caring professors who have known my name and appreciated my insights. There will always be disappointments wherever you end up, but I know I will always have nothing but fond college memories, long after I have moved on."

The College Prowler Take On...
Overall Experience

Most Pepperdine students are happy with the college they picked, their minor critiques of particulars giving way to an overall appreciation of the experience and benefits Pepperdine has granted them that no other school could. Students who don't gush forth wholehearted and unwavering words of love usually cite the school's size and social climate as the source of whatever dissatisfactions they may have. When people decide to transfer from Pepperdine, it isn't because of the lack of dining halls and parking availability, or some qualms they have about student housing; it's because of the other Pepperdine students and the community environment they create. For example, some religious students are dismayed to discover that many don't share their Christian enthusiasm. Others, in contrast, find the Christian atmosphere to be overwhelming.

Many students complain that the high schools they attended were larger and less strict than Pepperdine, with more to do on the weekends, while others with similar high school experiences find Pepperdine a welcome respite. And while some find the small campus and even smaller student population comforting, others find that Pepperdine's quaintness inhibits their growth and restricts their social life. There's nothing small, though, about the 125-foot cross that stands at the forefront of the Malibu campus the job of which is to proclaim loudly and clearly that Pepperdine's mission is not merely academic.

Ultimately, Pepperdine's considerable Christian affiliation defines it as a school. More specifically, it's the interaction between the religious emphasis and seemingly contradictory elements—luxury automobiles, non-Christian students, high heels and mini-skirts, a broad liberal arts education with its overwhelming price tag, the desire to let loose and party once in a while—that makes Pepperdine a dynamic and truly unique environment. The most amazing thing about Pepperdine may be that it has managed to hold onto its religious inclinations while still maintaining an excellent academic reputation. The University's mission statement affirms that "the educational process may not, with impunity, be divorced from the divine process." This language contrasts markedly with the prevailing public opinion that religion and academic rigor simply don't mix, and it highlights Pepperdine's willingness to approach higher education in unconventional ways. In the end, Pepperdine is a small Christian school that really wants its students to grow into people who might make the world a better place. It is not for everyone, but it offers plenty of rewards to those willing to take advantage of the educational and spiritual environment that is, after all, the reason they built Pepperdine in the first place.

The Inside Scoop

The Lowdown On...
The Inside Scoop

Pepperdine Slang:

Know the slang, know the school. The following is a list of things you really need to know before coming to Pepperdine. The more of these words you know, the better off you'll be.

The AC – The Appleby Center, home to the social science people.

The 'Bu – What locals call Malibu.

The CAC – The Cultural Arts Center. Artists, English majors, and would-be historians and teachers all congregate here for the bulk of their classes.

The Caf – The Waves Café, the only cafeteria on campus.

The CCB – The relatively new Center for Communication and Business, where communications and business majors spend the bulk of their time. It's up the hill a ways from central campus, which means that getting to class in the CCB, right after a class down the hill, can be a hurried and grueling endeavor.

➜

Convo – Every Wednesday at 10 a.m., students gather in Firestone Fieldhouse to listen to guest speakers and learn about campus events in order to fulfill their mandatory half-unit "convo credit," or convocation credit. You must attend fourteen convocations per semester to get an A.

Greek Row – The five freshman dorms located farthest from central campus, with Greek letters for names instead of numbers.

The HAWC – Pronounced "Hawk," this is the 24-hour student recreation center, with a pool table, a Ping-Pong table, a computer lab, a coffee shop, and places to study.

The Inn – The Malibu Inn, a popular bar just down the road.

Malibu Yo' – Malibu Yogurt, every female student's favorite frozen yogurt shop.

OneStop – If you need to do anything—from paying your bills to changing your major to contesting a grade—OneStop is the place to go. It's located in the TAC.

PCH – Pacific Coast Highway.

The "Peppervine" – Pepperdine's rampant rumor mill.

The Stinkies – Malibu Canyon Village Apartments, nicknamed for their persistent sewage odor.

The TAC – The Thornton Administrative Center, where the top-dog administrators have their offices and where students usually go to sort out financial or academic matters.

The TCC – The Tyler Campus Center, which houses the Rockwell Dining Center, the Sandbar, the Career Center, and various other resources for students.

TechDeck – The people to see if you need software, or have any technology-related questions.

UM – University Ministries.

Wave of the Week – During Wednesday convo, one Pepperdine kid is always announced as the new "Wave of the Week," Waves being the school mascot. Sororities, fraternities, and other organizations frequently nominate one of their own for this highly-coveted honor.

Things I Wish I Knew Before Coming to Pepperdine

• Surfing is hard.

• They really are serious about the whole religion thing.

• Wearing white socks with black sandals and shorts is considered unacceptable.

• Getting up and going to convo at 10 a.m. on Wednesdays is a harder feat to accomplish than it would seem.

• Many Californians aren't sure where Oregon is. I may as well have been Canadian.

Tips to Succeed at Pepperdine

• Take advantage of the international programs. If possible, spend a whole year somewhere. You won't regret it.

• If you decide to join a fraternity or sorority, be aware that Greek life will demand a lot of your time and energy; during pledge week, it is very easy to tell which freshmen are pledging, as they are the ones nodding off in your 8 a.m. classes.

• Be sociable. Pepperdine students are, on average, very friendly, so if you're not afraid to be a little gregarious, you will make friends in a hurry.

• As with any other school, to succeed academically requires that you know—or learn quickly—how to balance your time and resist the temptation to, for example, hit the bars every night of the week.

• Strike up good relationships with your professors, especially the ones teaching your major courses, immediately. Simply put, you will do better in their courses if you do. Also, it's good to build contacts for when you need advice or recommendations.

• If you're not Christian or not particularly religious, know that Pepperdine does not take its Christian mission statement lightly. Don't be surprised, for example, that you need to take three semesters of religion instruction. And don't be annoyed by all the religious fervor on campus, because, after all, an awful lot of students choose Pepperdine specifically because of its Christian affiliation.

- Take the Great Books Colloquium in lieu of a freshman seminar course. It's a four-semester obligation, but it satisfies a number of GE credits and is excellent preparation for the tougher courses you'll face as an upperclassman. It will help you immensely to think, discuss, argue, and write like a college student.

Pepperdine Urban Legends

The giant cross that stands out in front of Pepperdine, and which was built to light up at night, is now forever dimmed because of the protests of Barbra Streisand. The story goes that after the Phillips Theme Tower (which houses the cross) was first built, Pepperdine lit it up like a Christian beacon to the world, but the light kept disturbing Streisand's slumber at night. She supposedly complained to the Malibu City Council, which compelled Pepperdine to turn out the lights, and which gave us yet another reason to dislike Barbra Streisand.

School Spirit

Some students have oodles of school spirit. Others just don't. Those who have it tend to be fraternity and sorority members, student council types, or otherwise extraordinarily enthusiastic personalities.

Traditions

AWOL

The Alumni Association sponsors a week-long sendoff, called "A Week Of Leaving," for graduating seniors each April. Perks for seniors include free barbecue meals around noon and little trinkets and Pepperdine memorabilia so that you never forget where you went to college. The Alumni Association also uses this week to get the soon-to-be-alumni involved in the association's activities.

The Freedom Wall

Outside the Tyler Campus Center is a large corkboard on which students air their grievances or post their opinions on political, social, or academic issues. The "Freedom Wall" is supposed to foster intellectual debate, but mainly people start silly arguments or post dumb cartoons on it.

Homecoming

Since there is no football team, Homecoming events center around the basketball teams. The events are a means of coaxing alumni and friends of Pepperdine to come visit their alma mater, relive their youth, and then go home and send Pepperdine some more donations.

Midnight Madness

Probably the single most popular tradition at Pepperdine, Midnight Madness is an annual way of getting students together to pump themselves, and each other, up for basketball season. At 12 a.m. on the first day—well, night—that the men's and women's basketball teams become eligible to start practicing for the upcoming season, students pack the gym in the Firestone Fieldhouse to watch both teams take to the court for their first "practice." Organizers further bribe students by inviting movie stars such as Adam Sandler, Rob Schneider, David Duchovny, and others to challenge the women's team. Before midnight, the organizers put together little skits and spectacles to keep the crowd amused while everyone waits for the primary festivities.

Midnight Yelling

Although quiet hours in the dorms officially last for 24 hours a day during finals, dorm dwellers typically celebrate the midnight hour on each night of finals week by yelling and screaming in unison. Yes, it's pretty dumb. Sometimes a group of guys will run around outside in various states of undress. This is as wild as Pepperdine gets, folks.

Songfest

Pepperdine's version of a Spring Sing, this is a musical competition held each spring, with guest judges—usually minor TV celebrities—deciding which group of singing and dancing students wins.

Finding a Job or Internship

The Lowdown On...
Finding a Job or Internship

Pepperdine's Career Center, located in the Tyler Campus Center, exists to help Pepperdine students get the internships they need to graduate and to prepare them for careers after college. Often students find their mailboxes crammed with Career Center brochures and pamphlets inviting them to etiquette dinners, resume-building workshops, and job fairs. Pepperdine isn't going to go out of its way to find its students jobs, though; it's up to you to start the ball rolling by contacting the Career Center and starting the search for good internships.

Advice

Get in touch with the Career Center people early on (they're very approachable), and take advantage of what they can teach you, for free, about how to find an internship and present yourself to employers. Enlist the help of the Writing Center's tutors as you put together your resume; they can also help you polish business documents and application essays.

(Advice, continued)

The career and internship fairs on campus generally do not offer an enormous spectrum of job options, but be sure to attend, just in case. Also, use your free MonsterTRAK account, courtesy of Pepperdine, and check out what local job postings are available in the Career Center's Resource Room.

Career Center Resources and Services

Assessments

Campus employment

Career and internship fairs

Career Center Workshop Series

Graduate school advising

Help with resumes, cover letters, and references

Interview preparation

Major-specific job search

MonsterTRAK

The Resource Room

Grads Who Enter the Job Market Within

6 Months: 50%

1 Year: 75%

Alumni

The Lowdown On...
Alumni

Web Site:
www.pepperdine.edu/alumni

E-Mail:
alumni@pepperdine.edu

Office:
Alumni Services Office
(800) 767-2586 (ext. 2)
(310) 506-6190
Fax: (310) 506-4227

Services Available:
Alumni card

Alumni online directory

Discounts on movie tickets, theme parks, parking at LAX, car rentals, Smothers Theatre tickets, and most purchases at the Pepperdine bookstore

Free e-mail at *pepalum.com*

Free subscription to *Pepperdine Voice*

Kaplan Graduate School prep courses

Malibu campus parking sticker

➜

Major Alumni Events:

AWOL

Class reunions

Homecoming

Alumni Publications:

Pepperdine Voice –
This magazine comes out
twice a year and is free for
alumni and students.

Did You Know?

Famous PU Alumni

Rob Blagojevich (JD '83) – Governor of Illinois

Steven Baldwin (Class of '79) – Executive Director,
Council for National Policy

Dain Blanton (Class of '94) – 2000 Olympic gold
medalist in beach volleyball

Richard Carlson (PhD '83) – Author of *Don't Sweat the Small Stuff*

Doug Christie (Class of '93) – Plays for the Sacramento Kings

Bob Ctvrtlik (Class of '85) – 1988 Olympic gold medalist
in volleyball

Kim Fields (Class of '90) – "Tootie" on TV's *The Facts of Life*

Brad Gilbert (Class of '82) – Former championship tennis player
and Andre Agassi's coach

Jason Gore (Class of '00) – Walker Cup Team and PGA
Tour member

James K. Hahn (JD '72) – Mayor of Los Angeles

Dennis Johnson (Class of '76) – NBA Hall of Famer & LA
Clippers coach

Montell Jordan (Class of '91) – R&B recording artist

Jami Miscik (Class of '80) – Director of the Office of International
Affairs, CIA

Tia and Tamera Mowry (Class of '03) – Stars of TV's *Sister, Sister*

Eric Christian Olsen (Didn't graduate) – The young Lloyd
Christmas in *Dumb and Dumberer*

Todd R. Platts (JD '83) – U.S. Senator from Texas

Jessica Rivera (Class of '96) – Soprano opera singer

Bill Weir (Class of '90) – Sportscaster

Randy Wolf (Class of '97) – Plays for the Philadelphia Phillies

Student Organizations

Accounting Society

Advertising Club

African Alliance

Alpha Delta Sigma

Amnesty International

Armenian Student Association

Asian Student Association (ASA)

Black Student Union (BSU)

Bridge Club

College Republicans

Communication Association

Conglomerate of Ameliorators at Pepperdine (CAP)

Cultural Italian American Organization (CIAO)

Dance In Flight

Dance Team

Debate Club

East Coast Club

Entertainment Business Network

Feminist Forum

Golden Key (National Honors Society)

Habitat for Humanity

Hawaii Club

International Justice Mission

Latino Student Association (LSA)

New Music Ensemble

Ohio Club

Pepperdine Ambassadors Council

Pepperdine Film Study Initiative

Pepperdine Improv Troupe

Pepperdine International Club

Pepperdine Rotaract

Phi Alpha Delta (Pre-Law Society)

Phi Delta Epsilon (Pre-Med Society)

Pi Delta Phi (French Honors Society)

Pre Dental Club

Psi Chi (Psychology National Honorary Society)

Public Relations Student

Society of America (PRSSA)

Real Estate Informational Society (REIS)

Riptide – Spirit organization

Service for Life

Sigma Delta Pi (Spanish Honor Society)

Sign Language Club

Society for Human Resource and Management (SHRM)

Sports Medicine Club

Student Alumni Organization (SAO)

Student Dietetic Association (SDA)

Students in Free Enterprise (SIFE)

Swashbuckler Society

Table Tennis Club

Texans in California

Willy the Waves Chess Club

Young Democrats

Young Life

The Best & Worst

The BEST Things About Pepperdine

1	The view
2	International programs
3	Class sizes
4	Professors
5	Attractive people
6	London Broil in the Caf
7	Great Books program
8	The dorms
9	Weather
10	Location

The WORST Things About Pepperdine

1 Overly strict RAs

2 The less-than-perfect library

3 The lack of diversity

4 Monotonous and expensive nightlife

5 Lack of parking

6 Stairs, stairs, and more stairs

7 The anti-intellectual atmosphere

8 Long commutes

9 Convocation

10 The malicious "Peppervine"

Visiting

The Lowdown On...
Visiting

Hotel Information:

In Malibu

Casa Malibu Inn
22752 Pacific Coast Hwy.,
Malibu
(800) 831-0858
(310) 456-2219
Distance from Campus:
7 minutes
Price Range: $99–$329

Malibu Beach Inn
22878 Pacific Coast Hwy.,
Malibu
(310) 456-6444
(800) 4-MALIBU
www.malibubeachinn.com
Distance from Campus:
5 minutes
Price Range: $200–$570

→

Malibu Country Inn

6506 Westward Beach Rd.,
Malibu

(310) 457-9622

Distance from Campus:
10 minutes

www.malibucountryinn.com

Price Range: $140–$265

Through the Canyon:

Hampton Inn

30255 Agoura Rd.,
Agoura Hills

(818) 597-0333

www.hamptoninn.com

Distance from Campus:
22 minutes

Price Range: $99–$149

Hilton Woodland Hills

6360 Canoga Ave.,
Woodland Hills

(818) 595-1000

(800) 922-2400

www.hiltonwh.com

Distance from Campus:
25 minutes

Price Range: $90–$250

Hyatt Westlake Plaza

880 S. Westlake Blvd.,
Westlake Village

(805) 557-1234

Distance from Campus:
20 minutes

Price Range: $99–$139

Renaissance Agoura Hills

30100 Agoura Rd.
Agoura Hills

(818) 707-1220

www.renaissancehotels.com

Distance from Campus:
20 minutes

Price Range: $169

Warner Center Marriott

21850 Oxnard St., Woodland
Hills

(818) 887-4800

*www.marriott.com/
marriott/laxwc*

Distance from Campus:
25 minutes

Pepperdine rate: $85

Westlake Village Inn

31943 Agoura Road,
Westlake Village

(800) 535-9978

(818) 889-0230

Distance from Campus:
20 minutes

Pepperdine parent rates:
$125–$175

Regular Price Range:
$165–$395

In LA:

The Brentwood Inn

12200 Sunset Blvd.,
Los Angeles

(800) 840-3808

www.thebrentwood.com

(The Brentwood Inn, continued)

Distance from Campus:
30 minutes

Price Range: $140–$150

The Georgian

1415 Ocean Ave.,
Santa Monica

(800) 538-8147

(310) 395-9945

www.georgianhotel.com

Distance from Campus:
20 minutes

Price Range: $180–$300

Holiday Inn CITY Center (Convention Center)

1020 S Figueroa,
Los Angeles

(310) 476-6411

www.ichotelsgroup.com

Distance from Campus:
20 minutes

Pepperdine rate: $105

Take a Campus Virtual Tour

www.pepperdine.edu/virtualtour

To Schedule a Group Information Session or Interview

Call the admissions office at (310) 506-4392 to set up an appointment, anytime between May and January 15.

Campus Tours

Hour-long campus tours are available Monday through Friday and start on the hour, every hour between 9:00 a.m. and 3:00 p.m.

Overnight Visits

Unfortunately, Pepperdine does not offer overnight visits for prospective students.

Directions to Campus

Driving from the North

- From the Ventura Freeway (Highway 101) North, exit onto Las Virgenes.
- Turn left on Las Virgenes, which becomes Malibu Canyon Road.
- Follow Malibu Canyon Road through the canyon for about 10 miles.
- Turn right onto Seaver Drive.

Driving from the South

- From the I-405 North, merge onto the I-10 (Santa Monica Freeway) West toward Santa Monica.
- The 10 becomes Highway 1, or Pacific Coast Highway.
- Follow Pacific Coast Highway northwest along the coast for 13 miles.
- Turn right onto Malibu Canyon Road.
- Turn left onto Seaver Drive.

Driving from the East

- Take I-10 (Santa Monica Freeway) west to the end, where it becomes the Pacific Coast Highway (Highway 1).
- Continue along Pacific Coast Highway for 13 miles.
- Turn right onto Malibu Canyon Road.
- Turn left onto Seaver Drive.

Driving from the West

- Take Highway 101 South toward the Los Angeles Exit at Lost Hills.
- Turn right on Lost Hills Road.
- Take another right on Las Virgenes, which becomes Malibu Canyon Road.
- Follow Malibu Canyon Road through the canyon for about 10 miles.
- Turn right onto Seaver Drive.

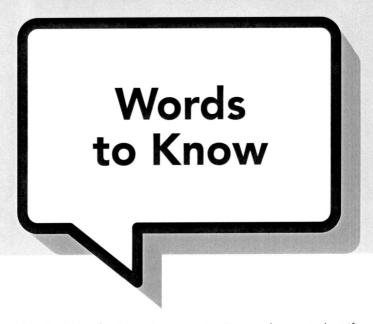

Words to Know

Academic Probation – A suspension imposed on a student if he or she fails to keep up with the school's minimum academic requirements. Those unable to improve their grades after receiving this warning can face dismissal.

Beer Pong/Beirut – A drinking game involving cups of beer arranged in a pyramid shape on each side of a table. The goal is to get a ping-pong ball into one of the opponent's cups by throwing the ball or hitting it with a paddle. If the ball lands in a cup, the opponent is required to drink the beer.

Bid – An invitation from a fraternity or sorority to 'pledge' (join) that specific house.

Blue-Light Phone – Brightly-colored phone posts with a blue light bulb on top. These phones exist for security purposes and are located at various outside locations around most campuses. In an emergency, a student can pick up one of these phones (free of charge) to connect with campus police or a security escort.

Campus Police – Police who are specifically assigned to a given institution. Campus police are typically not regular city officers; they are employed by the university in a full-time capacity.

Club Sports – A level of sports that falls somewhere between varsity and intramural. If a student is unable to commit to a varsity team but has a lot of passion for athletics, a club sport could be a better, less intense option. Even less demanding, intramural (IM) sports often involve no traveling and considerably less time.

Cocaine – An illegal drug. Also known as "coke" or "blow," cocaine often resembles a white crystalline or powdery substance. It is highly addictive and dangerous.

Common Application – An application with which students can apply to multiple schools.

Course Registration – The period of official class selection for the upcoming quarter or semester. Prior to registration, it is best to prepare several back-up courses in case a particular class becomes full. If a course is full, students can place themselves on the waitlist, although this still does not guarantee entry.

Division Athletics – Athletic classifications range from Division I to Division III. Division IA is the most competitive, while Division III is considered to be the least competitive.

Dorm – A dorm (or dormitory) is an on-campus housing facility. Dorms can provide a range of options from suite-style rooms to more communal options that include shared bathrooms. Most first-year students live in dorms. Some upperclassmen who wish to stay on campus also choose this option.

Early Action – An application option with which a student can apply to a school and receive an early acceptance response without a binding commitment. This system is becoming less and less available.

Early Decision – An application option that students should use only if they are certain they plan to attend the school in question. If a student applies using the early decision option and is admitted, he or she is required and bound to attend that university. Admission rates are usually higher among students who apply through early decision, as the student is clearly indicating that the school is his or her first choice.

Ecstasy – An illegal drug. Also known as "E" or "X," ecstasy looks like a pill and most resembles an aspirin. Considered a party drug, ecstasy is very dangerous and can be deadly.

Ethernet – An extremely fast Internet connection available in most university-owned residence halls. To use an Ethernet connection properly, a student will need a network card and cable for his or her computer.

Fake ID – A counterfeit identification card that contains false information. Most commonly, students get fake IDs with altered birthdates so that they appear to be older than 21 (and therefore of legal drinking age). Even though it is illegal, many college students have fake IDs in hopes of purchasing alcohol or getting into bars.

Frosh – Slang for "freshman" or "freshmen."

Hazing – Initiation rituals administered by some fraternities or sororities as part of the pledging process. Many universities have outlawed hazing due to its degrading and sometimes dangerous nature.

Intramurals (IMs) – A popular, and usually free, sport league in which students create teams and compete against one another. These sports vary in competitiveness and can include a range of activities—everything from billiards to water polo. IM sports are a great way to meet people with similar interests.

Keg – Officially called a half-barrel, a keg contains roughly 200 12-ounce servings of beer.

LSD – An illegal drug. Also known as acid, this hallucinogenic drug most commonly resembles a tab of paper.

Marijuana – An illegal drug. Also known as weed or pot; along with alcohol, marijuana is one of the most commonly-found drugs on campuses across the country.

Major –The focal point of a student's college studies; a specific topic that is studied for a degree. Examples of majors include physics, English, history, computer science, economics, business, and music. Many students decide on a specific major before arriving on campus, while others are simply "undecided" until declaring a major. Those who are extremely interested in two areas can also choose to double major.

Meal Block – The equivalent of one meal. Students on a meal plan usually receive a fixed number of meals per week. Each meal, or "block," can be redeemed at the school's dining facilities in place of cash. Often, a student's weekly allotment of meal blocks will be forfeited if not used.

Minor – An additional focal point in a student's education. Often serving as a complement or addition to a student's main area of focus, a minor has fewer requirements and prerequisites to fulfill than a major. Minors are not required for graduation from most schools; however some students who want to explore many different interests choose to pursue both a major and a minor.

Mushrooms – An illegal drug. Also known as "shrooms,"this drug resembles regular mushrooms but is extremely hallucinogenic.

Off-Campus Housing – Housing from a particular landlord or rental group that is not affiliated with the university. Depending on the college, off-campus housing can range from extremely popular to non-existent. Students who choose to live off campus are typically given more freedom, but they also have to deal with possible subletting scenarios, furniture, bills, and other issues. In addition to these factors, rental prices and distance often affect a student's decision to move off campus.

Office Hours – Time that teachers set aside for students who have questions about coursework. Office hours are a good forum for students to go over any problems and to show interest in the subject material.

Pledging – The early phase of joining a fraternity or sorority, pledging takes place after a student has gone through rush and received a bid. Pledging usually lasts between one and two semesters. Once the pledging period is complete and a particular student has done everything that is required to become a member, that student is considered a brother or sister. If a fraternity or a sorority would decide to "haze" a group of students, this initiation would take place during the pledging period.

Private Institution – A school that does not use tax revenue to subsidize education costs. Private schools typically cost more than public schools and are usually smaller.

Prof – Slang for "professor."

Public Institution – A school that uses tax revenue to subsidize education costs. Public schools are often a good value for in-state residents and tend to be larger than most private colleges.

Quarter System (or Trimester System) – A type of academic calendar system. In this setup, students take classes for three academic periods. The first quarter usually starts in late September or early October and concludes right before Christmas. The second quarter usually starts around early to mid–January and finishes up around March or April. The last academic quarter, or "third quarter," usually starts in late March or early April and finishes up in late May or Mid-June. The fourth quarter is summer. The major difference between the quarter system and semester system is that students take more, less comprehensive courses under the quarter calendar.

RA (Resident Assistant) – A student leader who is assigned to a particular floor in a dormitory in order to help to the other students who live there. An RA's duties include ensuring student safety and providing assistance wherever possible.

Recitation – An extension of a specific course; a review session. Some classes, particularly large lectures, are supplemented with mandatory recitation sessions that provide a relatively personal class setting.

Rolling Admissions – A form of admissions. Most commonly found at public institutions, schools with this type of policy continue to accept students throughout the year until their class sizes are met. For example, some schools begin accepting students as early as December and will continue to do so until April or May.

Room and Board – This figure is typically the combined cost of a university-owned room and a meal plan.

Room Draw/Housing Lottery – A common way to pick on-campus room assignments for the following year. If a student decides to remain in university-owned housing, he or she is assigned a unique number that, along with seniority, is used to determine his or her housing for the next year.

Rush – The period in which students can meet the brothers and sisters of a particular chapter and find out if a given fraternity or sorority is right for them. Rushing a fraternity or a sorority is not a requirement at any school. The goal of rush is to give students who are serious about pledging a feel for what to expect.

Semester System – The most common type of academic calendar system at college campuses. This setup typically includes two semesters in a given school year. The fall semester starts around the end of August or early September and concludes before winter vacation. The spring semester usually starts in mid-January and ends in late April or May.

Student Center/Rec Center/Student Union – A common area on campus that often contains study areas, recreation facilities, and eateries. This building is often a good place to meet up with fellow students; depending on the school, the student center can have a huge role or a non-existent role in campus life.

Student ID – A university-issued photo ID that serves as a student's key to school-related functions. Some schools require students to show these cards in order to get into dorms, libraries, cafeterias, and other facilities. In addition to storing meal plan information, in some cases, a student ID can actually work as a debit card and allow students to purchase things from bookstores or local shops.

Suite – A type of dorm room. Unlike dorms that feature communal bathrooms shared by the entire floor, suites offer bathrooms shared only among the suite. Suite-style dorm rooms can house anywhere from two to ten students.

TA (Teacher's Assistant) – An undergraduate or grad student who helps in some manner with a specific course. In some cases, a TA will teach a class, assist a professor, grade assignments, or conduct office hours.

Undergraduate – A student in the process of studying for his or her bachelor's degree.

ABOUT THE AUTHOR

Steve Pinkerton grew up in Oregon, but eventually forsook that state's damp embrace for the sunny climes of Southern California. More recently he's taken to the hills of Boulder, Colorado, where he's toiling towards an MA in English literature. In case you're wondering, his favorite books so far are *The Sun Also Rises*, *The Brothers Karamazov*, and *The College Prowler Guide to Pepperdine University*.

He'd like to thank the following for all their enduring support of his endeavors: Mom, Dad, Shannon, Tracy, and Grandma Dot. He should also give a shout-out to Cassie, who has the most greenish-gray eyes of all time. Lastly he'd like to thank Drs. Darrel Colson, James Thomas, David Holmes, and Lorie Goodman, without whom his appraisal of Pepperdine's academics would be significantly lower.

Steve Pinkerton
stevepinkerton@collegeprowler.com

California Colleges

California dreamin'?
This book is a must have for you!

CALIFORNIA COLLEGES
7¼" X 10", 762 Pages Paperback
$29.95 Retail
1-59658-501-3

Stanford, UC Berkeley, Caltech—California is home to some of America's greatest institutes of higher learning. *California Colleges* gives the lowdown on 24 of the best, side by side, in one prodigious volume.

New England Colleges

Looking for peace in the Northeast?
Pick up this regional guide to New England!

NEW ENGLAND COLLEGES
7¼" X 10", 1015 Pages Paperback
$29.95 Retail
1-59658-504-8

New England is the birthplace of many prestigious universities, and with so many to choose from, picking the right school can be a tough decision. With inside information on over 34 competive Northeastern schools, *New England Colleges* provides the same high-quality information prospective students expect from College Prowler in one all-inclusive, easy-to-use reference.

Schools of the South

Headin' down south? This book will help you find your way to the perfect school!

SCHOOLS OF THE SOUTH
7¼" X 10", 773 Pages Paperback
$29.95 Retail
1-59658-503-X

Southern pride is always strong. Whether it's across town or across state, many Southern students are devoted to their home sweet home. *Schools of the South* offers an honest student perspective on 36 universities available south of the Mason-Dixon.

Untangling
the Ivy League

The ultimate book for everything Ivy!

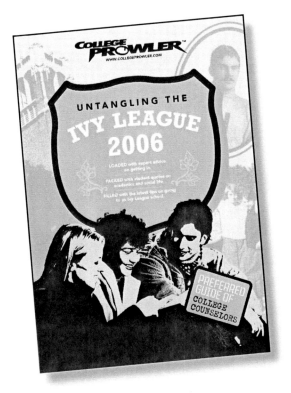

UNTANGLING THE IVY LEAGUE
7¼" X 10", 567 Pages Paperback
$24.95 Retail
1-59658-500-5

Ivy League students, alumni, admissions officers,
and other top insiders get together to tell it like it is.
Untangling the Ivy League covers every aspect—from
admissions and athletics to secret societies and urban
legends—of the nation's eight oldest, wealthiest, and
most competitive colleges and universities.

Need Help Paying For School?

Apply for our scholarship!

College Prowler awards thousands of dollars a year
to students who compose the best essays.
E-mail scholarship@collegeprowler.com for more
information, or call 1-800-290-2682.

Apply now at ***www.collegeprowler.com***

Tell Us What Life Is Really Like at Your School!

Have you ever wanted to let people know what your college is really like? Now's your chance to help millions of high school students choose the right college.

Let your voice be heard.

Check out **www.collegeprowler.com** for more info!

Need More Help?

Do you have more questions about this school? Can't find a certain statistic? College Prowler is here to help. We are the best source of college information out there. We have a network of thousands of students who can get the latest information on any school to you ASAP. E-mail us at info@collegeprowler.com with your college-related questions.

E-Mail Us Your College-Related Questions!

Check out *www.collegeprowler.com* for more details.
1-800-290-2682

Write For Us!
Get published! Voice your opinion.

Writing a College Prowler guidebook is both fun and rewarding; our open-ended format allows your own creativity free reign. Our writers have been featured in national newspapers and have seen their names in bookstores across the country. Now is your chance to break into the publishing industry with one of the country's fastest-growing publishers!

Apply now at ***www.collegeprowler.com***

Contact editor@collegeprowler.com or
call 1-800-290-2682 for more details.

Pros and Cons

Still can't figure out if this is the right school for you?
You've already read through this in-depth guide; why not
list the pros and cons? It will really help with narrowing down
your decision and determining whether or not
this school is right for you.

Pros	Cons
....	....
....	....
....	....
....	....
....	....
....	....
....	....
....	....
....	....
....	....
....	....
....	....
....	....

Pros and Cons

Still can't figure out if this is the right school for you?
You've already read through this in-depth guide; why not
list the pros and cons? It will really help with narrowing down
your decision and determining whether or not
this school is right for you.

Pros	Cons
....	....
....	....
....	....
....	....
....	....
....	....
....	....
....	....
....	....
....	....
....	....
....	....
....	....

Notes

....

....

....

....

....

....

....

....

....

....

....

....

....

Notes

....

....

....

....

....

....

....

....

....

....

....

....

....

Notes

....

....

....

....

....

....

....

....

....

....

....

....

....

Notes

....

....

....

....

....

....

....

....

....

....

....

....

....

Notes

Notes

....

....

....

....

....

....

....

....

....

....

....

....

....

Notes

....

....

....

....

....

....

....

....

....

....

....

....

....

Notes

....

....

....

....

....

....

....

....

....

....

....

....

....

....

Notes

....

....

....

....

....

....

....

....

....

....

....

....

....

Notes

....

....

....

....

....

....

....

....

....

....

....

....

....

Notes

....

....

....

....

....

....

....

....

....

....

....

....

....

Notes

....

....

....

....

....

....

....

....

....

....

....

....

....

Notes

....

....

....

....

....

....

....

....

....

....

....

....

....

....

Notes

....

....

....

....

....

....

....

....

....

....

....

....

....

Notes

....

....

....

....

....

....

....

....

....

....

....

....

....

Notes

....

....

....

....

....

....

....

....

....

....

....

....

....

....

Notes

Notes

....
....
....
....
....
....
....
....
....
....
....
....
....
....

Notes

....

....

....

....

....

....

....

....

....

....

....

....

....

....

Notes

....

....

....

....

....

....

....

....

....

....

....

....

....

....

Notes

....

....

....

....

....

....

....

....

....

....

....

....

....

Notes

....

....

....

....

....

....

....

....

....

....

....

....

....